T0193906

STILL STANDING
IN SPITE OF...

ELVIRA PLAVSIC

authorHOUSE®

AuthorHouse™
1663 Liberty Drive
Bloomington, IN 47403
www.authorhouse.com
Phone: 1 (800) 839-8640

Published by AuthorHouse 05/10/2019

ISBN: 978-1-7283-1095-4 (sc)
ISBN: 978-1-7283-1094-7 (e)

Print information available on the last page.

This book is printed on acid-free paper.

Contents

Preface and Disclaimer

I am not perfect—far from it. I am not throwing stones at anyone, and I did not write this book to be examined under an electron microscope. The language used is not from the vocabulary of modernism, objectivism, pragmatism, or any other -ism. It is written in a plain, simple, down-to-earth way so all can understand and relate to the message. Though sometimes I like to add some unorthodox sentences that are there to wake up our own way of thinking. The chapters are short for I am very aware that in today's culture, it is hard to find a time for a long reading.

The message is not here to destroy but to encourage, to give hope, and to elevate our minds toward a higher goal. It's a reminder that it's possible to grow and achieve the best in us, echoing the words *never give up*!

Was everything in my life *una bella serenata*, like the Italians would say? Of course not. The contrary may be the truth. But I refuse to dwell on it, and I'm focusing on the good.

The personal pronoun *we* is used a lot in this book, and that is for the sole reason of me not being there yet. But I am together with you on the path of getting there.

Am I repeating the same thing over and over again? Yes, but from different angles. I'm hoping that somebody will understand it better from one point of view, while others will understand it from another.

And we all know the good old Latin *repetitio est mater studiorum*. Repetition is the mother of learning.

The Rebuilding

I was nine years old when I saw the beautiful castle for the first time. Maybe I was not so impressed, for we had seen many castles before. All of us had. Then year after year, every summer, we would go there. When I was fourteen, I went there to be in a private boarding school. During World War II, the castle had been used by the government, and many things had been taken away from the property. Then it was taken away from the owners. After a long time, it was given to a private institution to take care of and use as a school for thirty years. It was taken good care of it during that time. But after that, it was abandoned again. I am very grateful to my parents, who sacrificed and sent me to that boarding school.

Looking back, I can say that, though we had something more special than the regular schools around, I did take it for granted. More than two decades had to pass before I realized the huge privilege I had being there.

We get things in our lives and do not even understand their value. Value increases with the passing of time, they say. How valuable are all the little things in our lives? Everything can be used to teach us something. We do not have to push ourselves to take lessons from things. But by cultivating grateful, cheerful spirits, we can learn to value the right things in our lives.

Things can be taken from us by force and against our wishes. But we can still value the things we have. We can still see how to use those leftovers for something good. Maybe it will not be appreciated immediately— perhaps never. We still have to do things that our consciences can approve of. And if our consciences did go off course, we should put that alarm on and sharpen them again. But that is another subject.

I remember the Latin classes that I loved and the language class that, let's say, I did not love. Nevertheless, I did well in both. Did I ever think that I would someday speak Spanish fluently and even teach in a bilingual

1

classroom? Thanks to the Latin, I learned Spanish very quickly. And where is the value in things we don't much like but have to do? My favorite thing to do for years was to write. I wrote letters, notes, and thoughts. Did it have something to do with my not so favorite subject in school?

There is value in every kind deed, smile, and encouraging word. There is value in the rain, though we prefer the sunshine. Let's use every brick thrown to us or at us or given to us, whatever the case may be, and put it into the buildings of our lives. One day, we may be surprised how tall our building stands because we converted all the bricks, using them to build and not wasting any of them.

We should always remember the ones who sacrificed for us, who trod the path long before us and show them our appreciation. We must remember those who taught us things we did not think so useful. But it turns out, they were.

An Old, Abandoned Castle

The castle stood there, and the people could guess its stories. Some accounts were told from mouth to mouth. Some were exaggerated, and some were just invented. It did not affect the basic structure at all. The people passed away, but the castle is still there. Its walls alone are witnesses to the real inside story. In our lives, there are people who guess at, invent, exaggerate, and pass stories. We can be labeled at childhood and bear those labels our whole lives, thinking that the wounds will never heal. But, yes, they can heal. We can have dreams of our own that nobody knows about for fear of being ridiculed, not understood, or maybe even rejected. So our dreams can stay inside in us, never being expressed or developed. Or maybe some could even be called dreamers for the crowd did not live within their walls. They could not understand their story.

Thankfully, we do not have to stay there. The obstacles in our lives can teach us the most beautiful lessons. The good things in life can teach us lessons. We can grow and decide which of our dreams we should follow and understand that we are responsible for our castle, not the crowd.

If the castle would be maintained all the time, it could for sure spare huge repairs that it needs now. Some of us were abandoned and not taken care of for a long time in various areas of our lives. But it does not have to stay like that. Surely, it would be so much easier if we could have had our "castles" maintained and perfect all the time. But we didn't. And some of us need huge repairs. Can that be an excuse to remain in ruins? Not at all. It will need some extra effort, extra willpower, and extra determination. But the excitement of the outcome should be a very strong fuel for that. And that outcome is the restored and renewed buildings of our lives—the castles that survived until now for a reason. There is a purpose for the building that was so neglected for a long time. It is going to be the most beautiful castle around.

Thomas Mann was a German writer especially known for his short stories. He received a Nobel Prize for literature back in 1929. His *Der Zauberberg* (*The Magic Mountain*) is a very interesting book that can be read like a parody of the changing times before the war in Europe. I am not necessarily absorbing all of his writings. Nor am I fan of his ideas about life. But he did write some pretty profound thoughts. For example, he wrote, "Forbearance in the face of fate, beauty constant under torture, are not merely passive. They are a positive achievement, an explicit triumph."

Here we are, standing in spite of fate and ready to achieve an explicit triumph.

Fear

The old folk story goes like this. There was a man who was very fearful. The night of his wedding he could not find the ring, so he asked his wife to come and walk with him. When he saw the moon, he said in a mocking voice, "Oh, moon, you are such a coward. Why are you hiding?"

The wife started laughing at his cowardice. She answered, "And you are such a wolf yourself."

When he heard the word *wolf*, being already filled with fear, he ran toward the house and accidentally stepped on the hoe that was left on the ground. The hoe's handle landed on his face, and he started yelling: "Woman, help me! The wolf is attacking me!"

Fear is a pretty good controller of our lives. It can induce us to make some terrible decisions or not make them at all. It can paralyze us or make us aggressive. It can put glasses with its signature on us, and whenever we look, we will see things through the lens of fear.

Fear has very good marketing and comes in many different packages. So, if we think we are not buying into it on one level, we may be grabbing it on the other.

We may fear pain, loss, failure, change, not being accepted, uncertainty—the list can be long. In my opinion, some portion of fear is necessary for our lives. Our bodies were made to have a healthy response to danger in front of us. Fear can make us alert when necessary. It can motivate us to flee toward a safe place—a case of a very positive reaction caused by fear.

Fear can be energizing or draining. But if fear is the leading cause of everything in our lives and our sympathetic nervous system is switched on and never turned off, we can experience burnout. And besides bringing us to make some wrong decisions, it can cause us to get seriously sick too.

Woodrow Wilson once said, "Fear God and you need not to be afraid of anyone else." Having some norms in life and knowing that we are to follow some moral principles can be very positive and eliminates the fear of the consequences of bad choices.

The fear I'm addressing here is the type that is making us sick. I'm talking about fear that drains us and leaves us almost unable to function. It scares us like a lion, because we know it's stronger than us and that we cannot go against it.

When I was in first grade many years ago, we read a little poem about a lion. There was a lion and the question was, What a lion? A terrible, three-eyed, and very angry lion. He ate whatever and whoever he wanted, until one day, a little girl did not erase him from the notebook with her eraser.

Many times, we cannot help but live in fear of that lion in our lives. It might be roaring around us and scaring us all the time. This is an invitation to take our eraser and just erase it. It was in our notebooks and we focused on it every day. We have to paint something else instead of that horrible lion that we just erased forever. It will not scare us anymore, because it is not there.

In the notebooks of our own lives, we have to take the erasers and decide to erase the lion; nobody can do it for us. Let's find the eraser and maybe get some coloring pencils to paint something beautiful—in the very spot where the fear used to be.

Half Time

This is absolutely a subject I never dreamed of learning a lesson from. Everybody around me loved soccer. Everybody around me watched soccer. Everybody around me talked about soccer. And I never understood the enthusiasm of the men who watched two groups of people running behind a ball from one end of a stadium to the other for hours. Now, I did like to know the result if the game was between two countries because all of us feel some kind of joy and pride if our country wins. Having my dear Argentinian friends far away from my homeland for sure did not make me forget my roots. These people were into soccer, cheering 100 percent. So I had to pick it up too. After the last year's World Cup, I even shed some tears of happiness (for a minute).

The first half of the game finishes after 45 minutes, and then the second half starts. The second half takes the same amount of time, 45 minutes. If there's no winner, we get an extra 30 minutes divided into two—15 and 15. Why did I break it down to the basic math? Because when we are in a certain stage of our lives, every blink of the eye counts. If there is no winner after 120 minutes, then each team gets five penalty kicks. The main focus of the two groups is to kick the ball into the goal—into the right one. You do not want to kick it into the wrong one.

Between the two halves, there is a very short time of not more than fifteen minutes but enough for the players to rest a little and review the game. It's a crucial time, focused on learning from the first half and preparing for the next. The players look briefly at a summary of their individual performances, focusing on things they did well and, the coach gives advice about where they need to improve.

Some of us are feeling far away from half time. Some are right on the border. And some feel that their game is almost over. I know for sure that

7

there are many who are discouraged for they feel that their lives passed away, running from one goal to another, but without any results. They are just getting used to the thought that this is the only way to finish the game—running from one goal to another, waiting for the sound of the game ending. They no longer aspire for anything more. Perhaps they did aim to hit the goal when entered the game, but for so long haven't seen any results. And now they don't have the motivation. The motivating force is drained, and lack of strength erases the firmness of will.

For all those dear people, I have very special news. Most goals are scored in the final forty-fifth minute of the first half and the ninetieth minute of the second half. Many times in the extra time of the game, the final goal is achieved. That is a pure statistic.

We have the brief half time to sit down and honestly evaluate our errors and mistakes; our failures and omissions; our blessings; and the grace, favors, and protection we received. We should be encouraged to renew our hope and to focus on the goal with enthusiasm like never before for we are now much more equipped than when we started the game. We did have enthusiasm at the beginning of the game. Now, correctly used, we have enthusiasm combined with the precious lessons we've learned, greater maturity, and familiarity with the strategy. We should burst with gratitude and enter the field determined to run and to win with joy.

What if we used up all our energies and the second half is finished with no positive results? A life wasted on running from one end of the field to the other. There are still thirty minutes of grace. Some extra happy endings came in games where the values (scores of zero) were suddenly replaced with the goal of a winner. Even if you can hardly bear the thought of fighting anymore for all you want is to live in peace the last moments of your life, what if I tell you that some world champions got that title because of the goals they reached in the extra grace time of the game?

Do not settle down before you kick the goal—the correct one. Did you know that, by the official rules, the goalposts must be anchored securely to the ground? We have to be sure that the goals of our lives are securely fastened on the goal line—not something fleeting and movable but, rather, an aim that's secure and sure. We're not here just to run from here to there but to have real-life goals.

There are people who make the goal in the beginning and stay there in a state of ease and triumphant euphoria, forgetting that the game isn't over yet. We can't give up the game just because we did something good a long time ago. Let us persevere to the end, and remember that there is no retirement in the stadium of life. We can win this championship, but we have to give all of ourselves.

We know that some players do not return to the second half. They are replaced by substitute players and don't take part in the remainder of the game. Did we start well and then get injured or taken out only to watch the game from the side? Will others finish in our place?

I know that not everything is exactly the same as in the real game, and I am not even getting close to incorporating the technicalities of the game. But we are not here to become professional soccer players. Rather, we are here to get a picture, from a different angle, of life.

One of the rules is that, if the ball becomes defective during the game, the Game has to stop and a new replacement has to be added. If we are running from here to there following a defective ball, we'd better stop and replace it. For that ball is the key, the only tool we have to achieve our goal. It's the object we're running behind, using our life's energy. Is it the right one? Or should we replace it with the one that is the best? We should stop to examine what we are following in our lives to see if those pursuits are bringing us closer to the goal and victory or just making us lose time and energy.

It is very important that a player does not wear or carry anything that may represent a danger to his or her fellow players. It's not just about scoring the goal but also about being considerate toward others. Some are going around in this life crowning themselves with the laurel wreath ahead of time, while injuring others with it along the way. They don't care about others or the final victory; they are all about themselves. And if they damage others, they aren't too concerned. Somehow, they ignore the first yellow card and the fact that there is a judge who can one day, after a lot of patience, lift the red one also.

Sadly, I see the extra exaggerations that I do not remember seeing many years ago. The players will roll and agonize in their hurt, waiting to get what they planned and then, in the blink of an eye, run again, more energized than ever—enjoying that their plan worked out just as smoothly as they designed it to. More and more people around us get their way through excellent acting and lies, and just an eye blink later, they display their handmade ornaments of glory. Our society is less and less sensible when it comes to the dangers of dishonesty, as long as the results are what they're expected to be.

Elvira Plavsic

The call is for all of us to examine the first half; make right the things that were not so good; leave behind the foolish and superficial; and, with steadfast determination and enthusiasm, go and do the best kickoff ever. We must enter the field and run toward the goal, knowing there are spectators around, many here to receive a legacy from us. We can show them an example of not giving up in spite of whatever happened in the first half, playing instead until the victory is sealed.

Gossip

N ow, gossip is a big subject. We grew up listening to small minds talk about people, as the saying goes on. But somehow, all of us are affected by that shallow yet profound trade. I guess we all have shared some very important information about others. Perhaps we were led by curiosity or were just taken away in the moment of such an important conversation. Some were only taking out their frustration about someone or sharing news.

All of us have been on the other side of the juicy and exclusive conversation too. The good news was shared about us, probably many times as well.

I am convinced that gossip should not be part of our lives. I am talking about those of us who've somehow concluded that our life calling is to solve other people's lives and, most likely, behind their backs. I remember a story from my childhood about two men who lived in the same place. Both had nice families. One of them started being jealous of the other. And secretly (as this is how this old trade is usually practiced), he started spreading false rumors about the other man. People believed what he said, and, if I remember the story well, the poor victim of the gossip lost his job, got depressed, and did not finished with the song "Happy Ending."

All of us have some falls here and there. But should our precious lives be marred by moments of destroying other people's lives?

The scariest ones were and are and probably always will be those with the smooth talking. I'm talking about the people who care for us but cannot sleep if they do not extract every bit of information out of us. Just think, how will they pray for us if they do not know every exact detail about our lives? Or how about the professional ones—those who would not go so low as to ask questions but who would take every secret out and spread it to humanity. Again, this is done behind the victims' backs for then the perpetrators feel quite accomplished. They almost feel that their résumé is improved by acts like this.

Oh, it doesn't stop here. How many families are broken and affected for reasons of behind-the-back problem solving? We should not forget that, throughout history, the weak have always wanted to show their power through the betrayal of gossip. They were the first to run to the authorities to say that somebody did something wrong. And, oh, did they exaggerate! Thousands and thousands were taken to concentration camps during World War II, thanks to the gossipers. And before that time too, in every cruel regime around the world, the same happened, passing the barriers of culture.

The human heart, if not cultivating the elevated and the pure, becomes a nightmare. Is it necessary to portray gossipers in such a bad light? Oh yes, especially because we live in this post-Freudian era, where everybody who does not have enough self-control and sense of importance managing their own lives somehow thinks it his or her duty to analyze others and maybe even label them for the good of the society.

We should never forget the good old story about the chicken who lost one feather. The other hen saw it and quickly clocked it to another. Didn't she hear that a chicken pulled out not one but two feathers from her own skin? *What?* she thought. *It is very important to notify others.* So important was the tiding that even the regular morning duties could be postponed for the beneficial task of sharing this horrible truth.

By the end of the day, the first chicken heard the news too. There were two chickens left without any feathers that day. "Oh my, how did that happen? It must be terrible! What a tragedy," said the first chicken, not recognizing herself in the story.

How do we stand in spite of it? First, by cleaning our own houses. We must take out our own tendencies to degrade others. We must decide on and stick to not saying anything that would affect others negatively. It is better to be the one who brings the good news, who cheers up, who is known to be confidential and trustworthy. There are so many bad things around us that focusing on them will cause this short life to pass in superficiality and triviality. We must exercise our decision to give people hope. I'd rather look back on my life knowing that I encouraged and lifted up instead of pushing down and covering with the dirt.

Are we doing it for some recompense? Absolutely not. Actually, it is so much harder to do the right thing. It's like swimming against the current, and in this case, accompanied by the sharks. But think about making it to the other side, where you can lie in a hammock in the shade, enjoying the sights. The beautiful white sand is not the perfect surrounding, for you will still need to do extra cleaning and washing again and again. But compared to the sharks, it is paradise!

I do not know why stories about gossip use feathers as a metaphor. Is it because feathers are so light and easy? Like gossip?

Here goes one you probably know. A priest was visited by a man who asked what he could do to clear up all the bad things he'd said about others. He was very sorry and wanted to do better. The wise man told him to take a bag of feathers, go to every house in the neighborhood, and put one in each yard. The man obeyed and felt relieved. Finally, he'd paid for his deeds and earned forgiveness from those he gossiped about. He ran to the priest and reported his accomplishment, but he was surprised by the answer. The priest told him that his task wasn't yet done. It would be done after he went back to every house and picked up every feather and returned it to the bag. It was an impossible task, we know. The winds of life spread the words we say farther than we can imagine.

Now, we're here to stand and not to despair and crumble under the weight of guilt. Today, actually this very moment can be the starting point, where we will permit the first bright beam of sunshine to enter in our hearts. For every negative comment we hear, we can simply turn away and decide firmly that there is a better place for us to be. If we have to cut out some people who pull us down, then let's do it, but with tact and love.

My mom told me many times that a person who will come to you with gossip about others will eventually gossip about you too. So let's start practicing saying nice things. If we can't, as they say, silence is gold.

The Marathon

A long time ago, I loved running. But not having the most enthusiastic companionship or the place for doing it at the time, I surrendered to circumstance. I admire my friends who didn't. One of them is still running, decades later. She is happy, and there is no conversation on this planet in which she doesn't make me laugh. She can cry with me and rejoice with me and pray with me, but in every circumstance, she somehow turns our sorrows, concerns, or mistakes into a good reason for a laugh. And the stone does not seem so heavy anymore. It does not matter how hard the battle may seem. There is a new ray of hope being born. A few of my friends love to run a 5K, and some run even longer races. One friend started running later in her life, and it became her passion. It just renewed her life. She runs marathons.

The marathon battle is not about the young man who runs to Athens for forty kilometers and dies from exhaustion with the last words on his lips being, "Νενικήκαμεν" (We have won). For according to Herodotus, the main source of the Greco-Persian history, the young man did run to Sparta from Athens before the battle, asking for help. And the Athenian army marched the forty kilometers from the battlefield to Athens. The legend unites these two stories. Here is how we have today's version of the young Pheidippides running to Athens from Marathon announcing the victory.

The Persians were extending their realm, and they silenced the revolt in Greece. The Battle of Marathon is extremely important to the Greek people because it was the birth of the ray of hope. It was the turning point in their history. The Persians were much stronger, and they outnumbered the Greeks. Athenians needed the help from Sparta, which they did not receive on time. So they had every reason to despair. Being outnumbered and without needed help from those who should have been there were reason enough to destroy hopes and bring down the vision of winning the battle. And a soldier who does not have faith in a victory has already lost the battle, even before it starts. Our minds are wonderful and magnificent strategy rooms—for the good or for the bad. It starts there—our defeat or our victory, our faith or our unbelief, our hopes or our despairs.

Athena and Sparta were the largest cities in Greece in that time, and they could count on helping and protecting each other from the enemy. But Sparta failed—for who knows what reason. Justified or not, the Spartans arrived at Athens one day later, when the battle was over. What can we do when our hopes and expectations are put on other people? When we rely too much on them and they fail us? Do we just surrender our lives and hopes and decide to be under the rule of dull, mindless, and soulless lives? Do we just surrender to the enemy of the real joy that invades our lives and let it conquer us? Do we have to subjugate our minds to the ideas of the enemy just because they are all around us and seem to conquer everything around, expanding its rule? Or can we still fight for our sovereignty?

The Greeks could easily have surrendered for that was expected. After all, many before them did surrender. Who are they to be different? Remember that it was not the empire we know about today; this was before that flourishing golden age of Greece. But here was the turning point in the outcome of this battle—in the decision whether to stay in subjugation or stand up and fight for freedom.

The Athenians stood up to defend themselves, and you can be sure that the battle was not won with hesitation. I do not know if they were marching with a beat of 120 or 180 steps per minute or even faster, but for sure they did not go around quickstepping. It was a very decisive battle. Every atom of energy was focused toward victory. We can be subjugated and defeated by life's destructive habits. But we have to stand up. Lost battles don't have the last word over our lives. The battle ahead can be the turning point. The things and people we put our full trust in can't always be here to help, but we have to stand up and fight for or own liberation from all the things that are pulling us down. We can't go wavering from here to there like in the ballroom. This is a battlefield.

Some just give in. They surrender and are dominated by everyday circumstances, never knowing or discovering how life could be if they would stand up for their rights—stand up and take off the yoke of subjugation.

If the Spartans would have come, the Athenians would have thought the victory was due to that union. But in this case, battling alone and winning gave them another look at the world—at themselves. They didn't need that reliance like they'd thought. They could stand up on their own. Sometimes we ask for help and gracefully do not receive it so that we can discover new potential in us we never dreamed of having. The victory raised the hope and self-respect in the Greeks once more, and it was the beginning of the long golden rule of the Classical Greek civilization.

It happened with just one decisive battle. How many of us will never know the glorious golden age because we gave up before that decisive battle? How many of us will give up because betrayal comes or because of fear or because we are outnumbered? What if the voices of our own reasoning or those of the people around us are claiming that the way of total submission to the current is the only answer? What if the years have passed away and we think that any change will be too much for us, that we are too old? Submission to the negative does not have to be the answer.

The Athenians did not look back. They stood up and valiantly fought the battle. They defeated the enemy. In spite of the obvious disadvantage, they won the victory. They were free—free to start on their own. The Persian invasion was broken, and the fear of Persia conquering Greece was ended. The victory created a sense among the Greeks that they must live free from outside influences, and they flourished like never before, developing their own criterion (a word that, interestingly, is still used in English but has a Greek origin—*kritē rion* means "to separate" or "to decide").

Do we have our own criterion? Or do we just repeat whatever the people around us are saying and doing? Do we value the gift of free choice we have, or do we let others think for us? Are we in some kind of semibondage to mediocrity and indifference? Just accepting whatever lands in front of us? Not deciding and judging what is to be used for good and what is to be discarded?

Just years after the victory, the Parthenon was built on the Acropolis, and the city became the center of art, culture, and intellectual development. Commerce was flourishing, and it becomes the center of the Hellenistic world, attracting intellect and curiosity, trade, and art from all over the world. All came as a result of one decisive battle, of not giving in but fighting. What is the cause you have to stand up and fight for so that you can start developing yourself to the full measure and flourish, being an example to others and an inspiration so they can see that it is possible to be free?

If the years have gone by and the burden of the wasted or ruined years is crushing some of us, we have to know that, in the battle of Marathon, there were many slaves. They were promised a different and new life if they would fight in the battle. They could have refuse the offer and escaped or gone over to the enemy's side. The slaves could reason that their lives were in bondage and now was too late to start anew. But thankfully, they did not, and they were free after that, having privileges and opportunities other slaves did not. Even if 99 percent of your life has been ruined, stand up and fight. The reward will be the freedom from the chains of slavery, and that 1 percent will be worth living better.

We all know what the chains in our lives are—what subjugates us—and what our battles are. For each of us, it is something different.

We can live free. We don't have to be subjugated by anything that is preventing us from flourishing and developing.

The Hurricanes

Hurricanes come unexpectedly, suddenly. They are large and scary. Merciless. We have just a couple days ahead of time to get prepared and to hope for the best.

My first encounter with a hurricane was many years ago in the Caribbean. Growing up in Europe, I'd never experienced one of the most intense storms that nature can produce. And then, suddenly, people became panicky, rushing, drilling, buying, watching all the weather channels available, and (in my opinion at the time) exaggerating.

They did explain to me that a big storm was coming, and they were actually drilling holes around their windows and putting up huge panels of metal or wood. Then the best part came—sitting in dark houses without a beam of sunshine, waiting for the mercy of the storm. Looking on the outside, it really didn't seem a possibility for me that something serious could happen. The sunshine and the complete absence of any kind of breeze was a sure indication that there was nothing to be afraid of.

Then it started raining, pouring, and flooding. The sound of the wind was scary. I knew it was the same as the horror movies, though I'd never seen one.

The next day felt like a microrepresentation of what Noah might have felt when he saw the land after the flood. Devastated. Ugly. Cloudy. Muddy. Broken and shaken. The beautiful flowers had disappeared, and the young plants once blossoming had been torn away, ripped away by force.

The side effects were just starting to expand their territory also. We had no electricity or running water. The not-so-nice smell that is the consequence of flooding was there too. The noise of the generators that every household had according to their means was everywhere.

And just in the case the next hurricane could happen, the people did not take the panels from their windows—for the whole summer. After such a devastating, sudden interruption of regular life, after brokenness, people did not want to risk losing something else.

I remembered the shutters on my grandmother windows, like the ones you can still see on the Mediterranean coast. She would open them every morning and close them every night. I never realized as a child the beauty and value of shutters. But now I was thinking that they were so much better than drilling holes every time a storm threatened. Now, that is my opinion. It doesn't have to be the right answer.

The message of this chapter is about our reaction to hurricanes in our own lives. Some of them are foretold by the forecast, and we have some rushing time to prepare. The hurricanes play with us. They have us in suspension. They can shred us to pieces or just have us there, sitting in fear, not knowing what to expect, and then decide to go around and leave us there—almost as if laughing at our fragile response to their monster-like control. How many of us were living in the sunshine hearing the forecast but somehow believing the threat was exaggerated? Perhaps we did believe the forecast but wanted to think that this storm would just pass us and leave us in peace. But we were surprised. We saw the young blossoming plants of our loved ones uprooted and broken. We witnessed the ugly consequences of the storm. We inhaled the smell of the flooded soil, where the clean and the dirty is mixed together and becomes filthy. We saw things that had been thrown to the trash and were not expected to float back to us.

Some people may suggest singing in such a hard time. And I dearly appreciate their effort to help. But as the wise man said there is:

> A time to be born, and a time to die; a time to plant, and a time to pluck up that which is planted;
>
> A time to kill, and a time to heal; a time to break down, and a time to build up;
>
> A time to weep, and a time to laugh; a time to mourn, and a time to dance;
>
> A time to cast away stones, and a time to gather stones together; a time to embrace, and a time to refrain from embracing;

> A time to get, and a time to lose; a time to keep, and a time to cast away;
>
> A time to rend, and a time to sew; a time to keep silence, and a time to speak;
>
> A time to love, and a time to hate; a time of war, and a time of peace. (Ecclesiastes 3:1–8)

And definitively, the time of the devastating hurricanes is the time of a deep cleaning. It's a time where we have to examine whether we want to drill the holes around the windows every time the danger comes and sit in the darkness without the beautiful healing sunshine or whether we want to think about the best solution for the next time. Maybe shutters? Maybe restructuring the whole concept of rebuilding our lives? We can add the good and take out the bad. We can learn to destroy the trash permanently—to burn it—so it will not float back to us.

We cannot change the hurricane, but we can change our response to it. I was reading about a whimbrel bird who flew into Hurricane Gert. Incredibly, she endured headwinds for twenty-seven hours and was able to fly at an average speed of only seven miles per hour and emerged from the middle of the storm.

But coming out was not the end of the story. The battle for life was still raging. She was pushed by strong tailwinds at an average speed of ninety miles per hour. And she safely returned to her staging grounds. Can you imagine the story of that little bird, if she could talk? She can't, but we can—not to talk for the sake of talking but to encourage.

We can share the testimony of the survival. It is possible to survive and clean up all the scattered pieces of our lives and see the new plants blooming again.

The Fiery Furnace

I am not a big lover of pottery. Quite the opposite is true. But knowing more about the way it's made makes me really appreciate the artists who make pottery. And I am calling them all artists—the old man behind the pottery wheel in the land of nowhere and the sophisticated ceramic artist of the finest name. All of them are artists. They all create something new, something useful, something unique out of mud. We can call that mud names and classify it, but it's just mud—dust mixed with water. All around the globe, in every culture, there is mud. It is universal, found all over the place, and cheap.

What makes the difference between the humble clay and the beautiful ceramic? A fire. Not just any fire but an extremely high-temperature fire. The soft, plain clay becomes stone-hard ceramic, never to dissolve again.

But what can an artist do with plain mud? What can a good potter make out of ordinary mud—the mud that people walk on, spit on, despise, and give no value to?

The clay is shaped and then put through a bisque firing through high-temperature heating so that it can solidify in order to put a glaze on it. That first shaped pot is called greenware and is very fragile, so it must be handled very carefully. It goes into a kiln, where it will be heated up slowly. Slow temperature rise is critical. At the beginning of the bisque firing, the last of the water is consumed out of the clay. If it is heated too quickly, the water will turn into steam, which can cause the clay to burst.

We enter the trials of life and, thankfully, many times don't even know what's ahead; if we did know, we would just burst. It would be too much for us. For the sake of mercy, we live day by day, having hope and slowly growing into what we have to in order to transform in our firing process.

The heat of the fire slowly rises, first to 660 degrees Fahrenheit. Then, when it reaches 930 degrees Fahrenheit, the clay is changed forever. The clay doesn't know it. It's still there inside the kiln, and the temperature continues to rise because just a change from soft to firm is not all we need. Did that poor clay ever imagine it would support the incredible heat of more than 1,700 degrees Fahrenheit? Never. But it was necessary. For just now, it is transformed to a point where it's not so fragile, yet it's porous enough to be ready to absorb the glaze that will be put on it.

We never dreamed in the stage of the clay that we would be put into a kiln, much less that we would support such trials as we did. And just coming out of trials isn't enough. Some people come out of them hardened, and here they stay—without compassion or beauty. Such a person is just one more survivor whose only difference from the clay state is hardness. Can it be that, after enduring such high temperatures, we will not finish the process and become all we should and are to become? The glazing will add that unique survival art after the high temperature's touch.

Glazing adds a safely sealed coating to the ware, making it waterproof and food safe. Just think about the endless possibilities of the patterns and techniques that can be put on that new creation. Glazing can transform ordinary ware into an extraordinary artistic piece. The color adds more options for artistic expression of each piece's uniqueness. How exciting to be a part of and a witness to the transformation from something ordinary, despised, and without value into such a masterpiece! Some will come out with a glossy glaze, shining around. Others will have a matte glaze. And while there appearance will be duller, they will still be masterpieces but in a different tone. One very important step to know is that, before putting the glaze on the pot, we have to be sure that all the dust is wiped away from it. If we want a glaze to be put on our exterior so that we'll shine, we will have to be sure that the dirt is taken away.

After the bisque firing process is over, the kiln is turned off. But the pots are not ready to run around trumpeting their experience. They have to slowly cool down. After our own firing experience, we often don't even understand all that we went through. We need a time of reflection. We need serious and earnest consideration. We need a time of questioning sometimes, a time of silence, a time of introspection. Sometimes time away from curious eyes and ears is what we need while gathering our thoughts and experience and getting ready to be glazed into new characteristics we never dreamed of having or developing. Then the beautiful glaze of the distinctive and remarkable new person can be put on us so that we can be the reminder of the nobleness that comes from the purifying process of the trials.

We cannot sit down and enjoy being out of the fire, for the complete beauty of the character must be added more. If we want to retain the liquid put into us, we need that glaze. We cannot be like some porcelain figurines, just waiting to be admired and doing nothing. We are to be useful pots. So for the pot to be waterproof, it needs the glaze and then again to go back to the kiln. It's very important that we're not loaded close to each other in that process, for the glaze would mix the colors, and it will not turn out good. Each of our experiences is unique. Our shaping cannot be made on a community level. We are to go through our learning experience on our own. Others cannot do it for us or learn in our place. And what was good for somebody else will not necessarily work for us also.

Again, the temperatures are rising, and we are brought into maturity. That's when the glaze and the clay melt together and become inseparable, rock hard, and impermeable to time and water. We are never again the same. The perfect harmony between the lessons learned from trials is the fusion of who we were and the glaze of who we became—maturity cooling down into a perfect beauty.

The Facade

In our daily conversation, the word *facade* came to symbolize almost a negative side of someone—like wearing a mask. But I think that facades do not have to always represent something bad. They can touch up something that is already beautiful.

In one country, I saw these houses that seemed to be very small at first. Some of them had these huge, almost out-of-place fronts. The facade was there to embellish, but somehow its disproportion just didn't fit its purpose. Then I saw in another country some houses where each looked completely different, with creative artistry on the outside. Each house had its own unique details that could take days to notice. When you stepped inside, the houses were just as interesting too. The front of the house or the facade was just the right indicator of what we may expect inside. For my taste, they were too colorful, yet they were beautiful. Then I saw these houses that I'd never seen before; they didn't appeal to my taste much. They looked small and too simple. Unusual. I even hesitated to enter. Once inside, I realized they actually were surprisingly nice and neat—not what I'd expected from the houses, which actually didn't have any facade. It was the same from every side.

Sometimes we can judge the book by its covers, but sometimes we can't.

I always like to wrap gifts. I love to give gifts that are not expected and are just a surprise. Sometimes they're valuable, and sometimes, they're just "a little nothing" (as I like to say). The only purpose of doing it is to brighten somebody's day or just to share. I love to make surprises and put gifts in the most improbable places, where nobody could expect to find one. I still remember a time when I was about six years old. We went to some party, and the hosts brought out this big beautifully wrapped box. When they opened it, inside was another box, and then one more until the gift was unwrapped. I think that inside was only a potato. It had a beautiful wrap outside and not a large value inside, but it was for the sake of healthy fun and laughter, which we all need in our lives.

The ideal combination should be a beautiful wrapping outside with a valuable gift inside, the outside evidencing the inside. Seeing a beautifully wrapped item can call our attention, and just merely observing it, we brighten up. It can be wrapped in a simple layer or can have more layers. Some gifts take more time to be unwrapped, adding additional charm with the special, unique details other gifts don't have. And then inside, the gift is always positively surprising too, with its beautiful arrangements and its particular style.

There are some strange people who do not want to give gifts but would rather put hay into a box. Yet wanting to be seen as very generous individuals, they make a beautifully wrapped box, and when you open it, there is neither a little nothing nor some valuable gift inside. Rather, you find a big nothing—something that shows you how low they value you. I've lived enough to see that too, especially around some big holidays.

Why would we wait for some milestones in people's lives to show them our appreciation? Every day is a gift—a beautifully wrapped gift. If we receive, why would we not give away? It doesn't have to be a gift in a box, but a word, a smile, a letter, or just a short note. I don't want to add a text message because I think we've became so superficial since this era of texting. But if that is the only venue, than text! Do so only if there is no other way around it, though. And I am sure there is. We should use our own creativity—or whatever is left after they've designed for us every possible response and we no longer think in a creative way.

I did receive the most valuable gifts in reused bags. The outside could not point toward the inside. I read some old books that looked like fossils, but I still loved them. I could learn a lot from them. Some of the most beautiful people around us are not always found in "beautiful wrapping paper." They come with wrinkles on their faces or spots on their worn-out hands. They can sit in the last pews and never be heard in public places. But it is their hearts, their souls—the value is not the facade. The value is the home itself, the interior.

Some do not have any facade. They are the same from all sides. The difference they can make is in the inside. Are they neat and welcoming? Do they surprise us with the inside beauty of character so much that we come to a point where we change our opinions about the small and the simple? The unusual?

And we will encounter along the road some small characters with a huge facade. Sometimes, it's because they just have that taste; for them, that's the way things should look. They are satisfied with their facade. They have almost nothing behind the facade that's original for all the houses around look the same. That exaggerated and flamboyant facade is all they have. It's a very pathetic and empty place to be.

We are responsible for our own homes, our own lives, and those affected by our decisions. How is our facade? Whenever we are on our life's journey, this is an invitation to check our front and our interior as well. Let's work toward beauty—first on the inside and, as a last step, the finishing touch of the inviting facade. We have to find our own pace and style. Work on the details that will be unique and creative. Some will work on the interior and, at the same time, on the exterior. Some will first take care of the inside and then turn to the visible. Whatever the case, it is all right.

Work on that smile and warmness. Add some details of decency and grace. Maybe add to it some wholeheartedness. The list is long, and the beauty of this is that we can work on it our whole lives, improving, adding, and taking out.

Then we can let people in without the fear that they will discover that our facade is all that we have. The facade will be just an addition to a beautiful building of our soul.

No Love

Vivre sans aimer n'est pas proprement vivre.
—Molière
(To live without loving is to not really live.)

Our life should be motivated by love—love for our neighbor and love for ourselves. Love for ourselves is interpreted not on the level of selfishness but on the level of wanting to achieve the highest noble traits of character that will make us as close as possible to the original plan, to being useful and a blessing for all, and to fulfilling that purpose for which we are created. We will love ourselves enough not to destroy ourselves with the low and the cheap but will, instead, elevate ourselves to the noble and precious.

Some of you maybe recall the words of Dean Martin's song "Hammer and Nails." I am talking about the first stanza only. In the same way, we can know about the construction. Choose the proper material and the best plans. Find the best ground and the best *paysage*. We can be experts, from carpentry and plumbing to framing and roofing. But if there's not a true love, home is not a home. The buildings of our lives should be well built and filled with love. They should be motivated by love—led by it.

The people around us should sense that we are not merely, coldly well organized but, rather, real, warm, compassionate, and filled with disinterested love. It is so easy to become selfish and just give up—especially if it seems that there is no encouraging response. But for our own sake, we should choose love. We should choose love that is true and not an impulsive, momentary, fleeting passion—love that has a calm and deep element in its foundation. This love looks way beyond the mere external

27

and is attracted by inner qualities alone. It is wise, refined, and of good judgment. And its loyalty is genuine and enduring.

Meša Selimović, author of *Death and the Dervish* (*Derviš i smrt*) wrote, "Everyone says love hurts, but that is not true. Loneliness hurts. Rejection hurts. Losing someone hurts. Envy hurts. Everyone gets these things confused with love, but in reality, love is the only thing in this world that covers up all pain and makes someone feel wonderful again. Love is the only thing in this world that does not hurt." We should balance toward that love that covers the pain and makes others feel well and wonderful again.

The well-known Latin saying *memento mori* is a reminder that all of us are going to die, like it or not, defying the idea of the creator or not. We will all die whether we are living in the most selfish way possible or in the most unselfish way possible. And we'll die whether or not we're ignoring death. Shouldn't it, then, be better to look back one day and know that we did not walk on this earth without purpose and guidance but filled with love and unselfishness, doing good and not bad, and helping others to see the ray of hope and love too?

We can do good and not be understood. The mob was always ready to go with the majority. When they needed personal help they seemed so touched by the love that healed them, but when selfishness and personal gain called, they were ready to crucify. The same audience is present in every stage of the spectacle—ready to praise and applaud or to throw stones and ridicule, depending on the personal momentarily gain or the loudest voices around them.

Love can be misunderstood and bruised. It can be thrown away and tread down. Love can be lied about and mocked. It can be unjustly punished and rejected. It can be imprisoned by the lovers of self. It can and should be left alone by those who do not care. It can cry alone in the darkness, where no one will see it and hide in its pain.

But love is still is greater than all that together and surpasses and resurrects and keeps on. Love finds new hearts and lives where it can grow and spreads, bringing life's fragrance that cannot be compared to any other.

The battle is harsh and unfair. Pure love can do nothing else but good. The tools that are used against love are not permitted for love to utilize. But in the end, real love, unselfish love conquers all.

Amor vincit omnia.

Discouraging Voices

Isaac Newton, according to many leading thinkers of today, especially physicists, asked the most important question in history.

As many of you know, Newton was born in England in 1642 and was a mathematician and physicist, as well as an astronomer and natural philosopher. And like every truly great person, he was humble. The story goes that, while he was staying at his mother's place, he saw an apple falling and started to wonder, If the apple is falling it is being pulled by some force, so what is pulling the moon also? Yes, this is a super simplified version of the heavy scientific words Newton used. All who want to go directly to the source can read his book *Principia*. Actually, if we think a little more, our lives are a lot like his third law of motion—action and reaction.

In spite of the high respect I have for Sir Isaac Newton, I am convinced that there is a much more important question in our lives to be answered than the question of gravity.

I do think that the question of our purpose in life is the most important. If we just go bumping from one idea to another and follow the major postmodernist philosophy that there is no absolute truth, then we are going to destroy ourselves because there are so many voices from so many sides that a lifetime is not enough to try them all. Actually, the very same Newton said that truth is to be found in simplicity and not in the multiplicity and confusion of things.

The three leading founders of the philosophy that says there is no absolute truth are all countrymen. According to the World Health Organization, that country is among the top countries for clinical depression. Our dear country is ahead of it. Too many voices are analyzing, solving, dissecting, finding new ways of "how-to," and giving lectures on everything and everyone. Living life as if there is nobody to give answers to is not *la vie en rose*. Actually, it is very hopeless and empty.

What if technology is the answer? It isn't. The country that is king of technology, with an extremely well-organized system, is at the top of the charts when it comes to the suicide rates. I don't want to mention the names of the countries I'm referring to, because the point I'm making isn't about the countries. Rather, it's about our concepts of the final answers. With a little bit of research, you can find out or probably you are guessing already.

Our society knows the answers to every problem—even to things that are perhaps not problems, just different perceptions. We are saturated with every form of philosophical and scientific answer and with a variety of educational theories, but confusion is on the rise. We can no longer go to our grandparents and ask questions, supposing that they've lived longer than we have and that they have something called experience combined with wisdom—because they do not have the certificate to answer a particular question. We have to go to an expert who is qualified by the books to give us that answer. And never forget; there are forms we have to fill out before we can ask the question. And we must sign them.

The Western world is leading, but thanks to technology, wars, and some other ways, the rest of the world is just behind—almost getting to the goal too.

Sound depressing? It is. But.

Do you remember the story of the frog who fell into a deep pit? His so-called friends and others came to see him. Looking from the top, they would say that his situation was hopeless and that he should stay there. Scientifically, there was no way for the frog to get out. All the measurements were there to prove it. The counselors were probably talking about the best way to remain there in the pit and get used to the idea that this was it. It is fortunate that the frog was deaf. Those who were giving their advice did not know that. So he would see their gestures and desperation. He saw them pointing and trying to tell him something. The little frog understood the message. He was sure that they were encouraging him to get out. How could he disappoint them? They were here to cheer him, to help him come out of the pit. He jumped and jumped. He used every bit of energy left in him. And finally, he jumped out. What a surprise for all those loud voices of discouragement.

This story is a powerful message of encouragement. We have to learn how to translate the negative and destructive messages into energy for us to jump out from whatever pit we are in. The pit of many voices should be left behind. We have a purpose to accomplish—a noble one.

I barely remember an old movie where everybody thought that an old man was deaf. The surprise was that he was not deaf; he had just learned to ignore his wife's nagging. Let us become deaf to the negative and purposeless around us.

My parents are of two different nationalities, and my grandparents on one side were in a mixed marriage too. I don't think there a word of similarity among all the languages represented in the mix. So my mom would tell me to go and say this or that to my dad in one language. I would tell him the message in his language, perfectly translated, not even thinking about it while I was walking. What a beauty of the brain and the thinking process. What a perfect master art. While I was walking for a couple seconds, my brain did the job. What a treasure to keep.

Nobody should think for us. We have a marvelous gift from our maker, and it is our brain. We have the perfect ability to process the ideas and to conclude for ourselves what goes and what does not go. That liberty makes us different and unique. It makes the world more interesting. Let's train our brains so that, while we walk from point A to point B, we just naturally translate the negative into a positive—from one language into another. After years of training, you will do this so naturally that it will be your nature. You will live a life with a purpose in the midst of the confusing voices.

Our Titles and Degrees

I do want you to know that I am very grateful to my parents for the education they provided for us. I am not against education at all. I'm very pro-education, actually. But I'm talking about the real kind of education.

I'm not forgetting that the paper on the wall is not what defines my character or who I am.

I always loved the stories about Abraham Lincoln. I don't know how much is made up or how much is the truth, but those stories were always about his humility. They tell how Lincoln didn't become arrogant and haughty, instead remaining simple, humble, and kind. Did he have a real job to do and great responsibilities so he could have an excuse not to be kind? Regardless of all the important work, he was still kind. Down in the valley or on the top of the mountain, he remained him. The paper on the wall did not make him who he was. And his paper was bigger than many of those we have or will ever have. More important, did that title and position make him talk to the people like an Egyptian pharaoh or was he more like Moses? Like the divinity or like a fellow man, one of the same flesh, who had a huge responsibility of leading his fellows? Was he understood and treated with justice? If I understood well, he was actually treated very unjustly. But he was himself. In or out of the White House, he was the same—kind, caring, and full of compassion.

One of my best friends has performed many eye surgeries and is very intelligent. But she never trumpets around about her profession. Of course, it is nice to be recognized, but remaining who you are in spite of your degrees is the greatest greatness—at least one of them.

There are many who remained erect and firm during hardships but, when tried on the level of human recognition, stumbled. Some even fell.

For me, it's very shocking to see how these times we live in are so résumé oriented. Many years ago, I was amazed to notice how a person has to praise or evaluate him or herself. We have become used to describing our own skills as excellent, outstanding, or even exceptional. Sadly, we start to believe that things written on the paper or screen are who we are. It comes that the person who does not have a mile-long résumé is not a full person.

It doesn't matter how many times I see this emphasis on the résumé only; it always reminds me of the words: "Let another man praise thee, and not thine own mouth; a stranger, and not thine own lips. " These words were written by one of the wisest men who ever walked on this soil. Yet due to his own self-exaltation and pride for the "skill" he possessed, he relied too much on his abilities to choose the path on life's crossroads, and he fell deep down. His case was almost hopeless. He spent the last years of his life in profound regret, trying to warn others not to repeat his steps.

I was amazed by the new names used to describe today's jobs. I think it's absolutely a stunning phenomenon! I actually almost applied for one job because the job sounded so scientific and so related to space engineering that it perfectly matched with my not-so-engineering résumé. Then the confusion started. Reading the description of the job, I found all these extra fancy and extremely important, flourishing words that somehow did not match with the salary description. I asked my friend for help. She is one of those who knows everything but does not go around with fanfare. She is just plain smart, a retired teacher. She's someone who doesn't need all those fancy words to describe the job of a secretary.

Who are we fooling? Do we need all these extra aerospace engineering words in an extra fancy presentation just to describe a job that our grandmas or grandpas did too? Do you remember the story, "The Emperor's New Clothes"? It was written down by Hans Christian Andersen, but it was an old folk story passed from mouth to mouth from generation to generation. We had to read it in our second or third grade. I love the message of the story. It is so timeless. There is nothing new under the sun.

A vain emperor cared about nothing but himself and promised a big fortune to those who made him the perfect clothing. Two weavers came, convincing the emperor that they had this new invisible thread to make a fine fabric. It was the newest, of course, state-of-the-art technology. Only the unfit and foolish or stupid couldn't see the thread. Only the educated could see it. That was how it was promoted. The false designers were pretending every day to sew, to measure, and to weave. But nobody could see the clothing. Nor could anyone see the fabric or the thread. Who would say that there was nothing on the king? That he was ... No. Nobody wanted to be perceived as ignorant or uneducated or against the latest in technology and science. So came the big day. The emperor led the parade with the subjects all around in the streets. And all as one they admired the emperor's beautiful clothing.

Of course, like always, those who were most superficial were the loudest in their admiration—until a child told the truth. The child just said what he saw—the emperor was naked.

Let's not be swayed by titles and degrees. Let's always thrive to the best we can be, staying humble and kind.

English Romantic poet Percy Bysshe Shelley wrote a poem "Ozymandias" in 1818. Ozymandias was a Greek name for the Egyptian pharaoh Ramses II. That same year, it was expected that the British Museum would bring home a large part of the statue of Ramses II. The head and the torso weighed more than seven tons. That's a lot for something we could call ruins. Once a mighty ruler, who with pride engraved in the stone how great he was, Ramses II was now nothing but a lifeless stone in the sand. The poem is about the frugal nature of power, which declines no matter how great the powerful consider themselves. Shelley wrote:

> I met a traveler from an antique land
> Who said: Two vast and trunkless legs of stone
> Stand in the desert ... near them, on the sand,
> Half sunk, a shattered visage lies, whose frown,
> And wrinkled lip, and sneer of cold command,
> Tell that its sculptor well those passions read
> Which yet survive, stamped on these lifeless things,
> The hand that mocked them and the heart that fed;
> And on the pedestal these words appear:
> "My name is Ozymandias, king of kings;
> Look on my works, ye Mighty, and despair!"
> Nothing beside remains. Round the decay
> Of that colossal wreck, boundless and bare
> The lone and level sands stretch far away.[1]

---

[1] Percy Bysshe Shelley, "Ozymandias" in *Miscellaneous and Posthumous Poems of Percy Bysshe Shelley* (London: W. Benbow, 1826), 100.

Not Having Worth

G old, in its purest form, is a bright, slightly reddish-yellow, dense, soft, malleable, and ductile metal. Gold is resistant to most acids. A relatively rare element, gold is a precious metal that has been used for coinage, jewelry, and arts throughout history.

Malleability is a material's ability to deform under compressive stress. This is often characterized by the material's ability to form a thin sheet by hammering or rolling. Gold is ductile. It can be drawn out into the thinnest wire. One ounce of gold can be drawn into fifty miles of thin gold wire, five microns thick. Both of these mechanical properties are aspects of plasticity—the degree to which its form can be altered but not fractured.

Pure (100 percent) gold is marked as having 24 karats. However, it is unusual to find a "24k" mark on a piece of jewelry because pure gold is a soft metal and is more likely to scratch and bend. Gold in jewelry is, therefore, often mixed with other metals to make it more durable. It is called an alloy—when it is mixed with other metals to make it more durable. Gold jewelry can be alloyed with silver, copper, zinc, palladium, and nickel to create different gold colors. The most common gold colors are yellow, white, rose, and green.

Yellow gold is made by mixing pure gold with silver, copper, and zinc. White gold is made of gold and platinum or palladium and can also be made with nickel and zinc. Rose gold, or pink gold, is alloyed with gold, copper, and silver. Green gold is mixed with gold, silver, and sometimes copper.

Depending on the added metal, the gold will have its typical property, or uniqueness. More silver will make it more greenish. More copper will call it toward red or add to its durability and scratch resistance.

Since we've learned here everything we already knew about the basics of gold, let's see how we can translate that knowledge to our daily lives.

Gold has always been associated with the worth. Depending on the future use of an item, the gold is mixed or not with other elements.

We all have the potential worth of gold. Some of us are still like golden nuggets, waiting to be discovered and processed. Borax and soda ash are added to molten metal, which separates pure gold from other precious and less precious metals. Now, if we want to be pure gold, we have to go through that process of refining.

Every person is at a different stage of the process. The only difference between us and the gold is that we can refuse to become refined.

We will not be the same at the end of the process. Some will choose to be alloyed with the different elements that fit their lives for better endurance and purpose.

My favorite gold is rose gold. It has that timeless elegance and delicacy in it. But that's me. It doesn't have to be your taste. You may love gold that is yellower or whiter. Perhaps you love greenish gold. Our tastes are different, and that is such a blessing. We do not want to be the same in all things—*as long as we remain gold.*

Being gold, we are unaffected by air, water, alkalis, and all acids except one mixture of hydrochloric acid that has its Latin name. We do not want to put attention on that word but, rather, on our strength. We can be hammered, pounded, and beaten or rolled out to unthinkable sizes. We can be compressed to high stress, but we remain gold. Our characteristic is to have plasticity. That means that, after all of the stress put on us, our form can be altered. But we are not getting fragmented or broken.

I was sitting at a concert in a beautiful hall. The lights were so perfectly focusing on the performers and the stage decor. For a moment, I glanced at my purse. My purse was a combination of black leather and gold—an imitation of gold that looked just like the real thing. At least that was what I was convinced of, until the eye-opening moment. I was staring at my purse, not understanding what had happened to "the gold." It looked so faded. It looked like some cheap plastic.

After focusing on a perfect performance accompanied by shine, my poor imitation was not so shiny anymore.

If we focused on ourselves, we would be probably very satisfied with our shine—authentic or fake. But if we focus on things that are better and nobler, then we'll realize we are not the shiniest element in this world.

The value of the gold is not in its shine. Fake things can be bright too—especially in today's world. There are so many imitations, so much glittering plastic. The value of the gold is in the mere fact that it is gold. It can be covered with mud, submerged under water, hidden in the dark—it remains gold. The shine just embellishes its worth and makes it more attractive.

Let us give worth to ourselves and others—and act according to that knowledge. We are refined, in different forms and colors, used for different purposes. But we are gold. And let's remember that all of us started being just a nugget.

Being A Simple Wood

If you ask me what nationality I am, I sincerely do not know. The older I am, the more complicated it is. I know in which country I was I born. I know whose citizenship I have. But the between questions are so complex. For not even I understood it well while growing up. I just knew that it was not so fancy to declare that you weren't 100 percent this or that. So I wouldn't speak one of the languages I knew in front of people who did not speak it. One of the languages I spoke became predominant because the first school I attended was bilingual, which added a third language. But then I was put in a school with just one language, and there I used the secondary language. I still remember lying in bed at nights at my boarding school and consciously deciding to think one week in one language, another week in a second language, and so on until the end of the cycle and then start again. It worked for years, and nobody knew it. Now it feels almost like being inducted to some kind of hall of fame knowing all the languages. I am so glad I was born where I was born for all the precious experiences along the path, for diverse people and cultures, for the blessing of living where I live now—and for the languages.

I have my taste and things that I love, and it's my hallmark. But at the same time, I believe that our experience should be enriched, without causing us to lose our direction and enabling us to stay true to our authenticity while expanding our horizons. One of the fields is music.

We love to sing in the car. That is our rehearsal room. Nobody can hear us. Depending on our moods, we can sing or just listen to the music or harmonize perfectly. Or some of us just pretend to harmonize (and I'm pointing toward myself). But most of all, we like to see what the newest songs are and for whose taste is that downloaded.

I would download some favorites and some not so favorites but from different cultures and languages. There is a branch in music from one of the places I grew up whose theme is that no time or distance can heal our antagonism. I just get sick listening to it. But I found one or two pieces from that genre that are bearable. So I added them to my downloads to listen to while I am driving (not in heavy traffic). There are some that are not on my "must accomplish" list, but I do it for my family.

Then there are the songs I always listened to and loved while growing up—the ones I could download hundreds of. They are in different languages, in different styles, played with different instruments, and from different cultures.

There are accordion sounds and trumpets; a cappella from the coastal area that is profoundly beautiful (*klapa*); violins with an orchestra; the lonely bouzouki, mandolins, or the clarinet; the sensible acoustic guitar; and the list goes on.

There are languages I can read and write and speak. Then there are the ones I can read and write but can no longer speak—gone with the wind. And there's one I can read but do not understand—maybe every hundredth word. We have the same letters that are very unique, but the spoken language is just very different.

The same instruments with their music can produce pleasure or displeasure. The music can be piano or fortissimo. It can induce happiness or sadness, nostalgia or joy, love or hate.

Just like we, people, can.

We are composed of the same material. We function with the same natural laws. A person living in the southern hemisphere and someone from the north have the same needs. The person driving the sixteen-cylinder engine car with a two-letter logo and the one pulling the rickshaw have the same need. The same cardiac muscle fibers compose the hearts of every person from this nation or that nation. People are not defined by their nationalities. They should be defined by their qualities. The same bouzouki that produces the melody that brings cheerfulness or beauty can induce an almost repugnant feeling with other kinds of music—at least for me.

The player who runs the bases fastest and the person in a wheelchair have the same needs. They need the same oxygen and water, food and sleep. They need to be loved and to be accepted for who they are, not for their accomplishments or lack thereof. A person who cannot run as fast as you or cannot see as well as you or cannot speak like you is still a person with a heart that is beating for something more than just to get his or her physical needs met. When surrounded with people who are weaker than you, maybe you feel good about yourself. But what about being around giants in their fields? Don't you feel a little insecure? Remember that next time you are tempted to put yourself on a higher pedestal.

There are a few who like to drive slowly through life, listening to *mandolinatas* while contemplating the sky in their cabriolets. And there are others who live the sharp, fast, and determined sounds of the Vivaldi's Four Seasons *Summer, movement 3: Presto.* I do think that they live presto lives while driving their five layers of paint shiny car. And there are the ones between. That is the majority.

The material is the same. It's not some big inventory of building materials or performing methods for the musical instruments. If we judge by the range, we have just five different ones and if we go by the material used to make them, it is just about the same number. Let's take the wood.

A simple piece wood can be made into a violin or a guitar. It can be made into a cello or a piccolo. How many different sounds can it produce? Let's take the violin. It has just four strings. But it can perform thousands of different songs in many different genres. The same violin can produce some scary and unbalanced sounds or the most beautiful, harmonious melody.

We can be just wood, lacking any external shine. But we can also become violins or guitars or cellos. We are the same in terms of building material, but we're diverse in our expressions, and therein lies the beauty of it. We can all be the same instrument; what will define us is not the shine or the name but the sound. We are what the sound of our soul is.

Knowing this, let's see the people around us not like rivals or like something inferior but like our family. Let all of us use our unique sound together with them to create a pleasant harmonious melody.

Injustice

This is an old folk story from the time of the Ottoman rule. A poor man had to take care of the Turkish judge's cattle, and he had one cow of his own there. One day, one of the judge's cows pushed the poor man's cow, and pushing back, the second cow killed the first.

The poor man ran to the judge and said, "Your cow killed my cow!"

"Did somebody push her to do it?" asked the judge.

"No," answered the poor man.

"There is no law for cattle. If she killed your cow, I cannot do anything about that," replied the judge.

"Oh, didn't you hear me, judge?" asked the poor man. "My cow killed your cow."

The judge quickly opened the book and said, "Let me see what the law says about it."

"Oh, no you will not. If there is not a law for your cow, there is not a law for my cow either," replied the poor man.

We could probably write encyclopedias about the subject and not even finish the introduction. But we're here to learn how to stand, not to hear more about the boss who is unjust or who never heard about genuine politeness. We're not here to hear about the lazy people at work who get promoted. Then there are the hardworking people who somehow remind us of slavery times because, no matter how honest they are or how hard they work or how much more knowledge they have than the boss / slave owner, which is often the case, they remain down. They remain used and misused, their lives slipping away and their dreams fading forever, while those who use them are growing—progressing, they call it.

The person who works hard is paid like a medieval peasant, while the feudal prince is feasting. Now, of course, we are a very enlightened society.

41

So we understand that people receive pay according to their titles, not the actual work they do. So why, then, would they work? That's the message to the young people—working, whether or not you work hard, will not pay off. Just study. Forget about manual work. It's not for humans. (I'm still waiting to see how we'll survive with all our degrees if no one is working hard in the fields, producing the food we have to eat).

Thomas Jefferson knew that truth. That's why he wanted that this country's main orientation to be agriculture and trade. The leading minds of this country's birth were learned in books and, at the same time, knew physical work too.

Will this chapter change the minds of people who love injustice? Probably not. Especially if they are sitting all day long planning and making more rules about how things outside should function. I guess Plato already knew it when he said that the worst form of justice is pretend justice. Perfect the papers on the annual, monthly, weekly, or daily reports and meetings.

What about the children who were smart and longing for love like every other child but were pushed aside for not fitting in? For not being good on the football field? Or what about the children who don't have loving parents—the children whose hearts long to be accepted but who are ridiculed? And what of those who have loving parents but are bullied for being too protected? What about single parents working out their souls while the other parent selfishly lives his or her life? There are those who are born on a point of the map that makes them feel superior to those born on another point. Justice in the courtroom should be decided with blindfolded eyes to prevent unjust dealings, but in truth there is a different blindfold— one that prevents the truth from being seen. We all remember the stories or some of us saw the silent reminders of the brutal holocaust from the Second World War. We've seen images or heard of the trains taking the innocent toward barbaric tortures while the betrayers feasted on their bounties.

Injustice is very well rooted and seated in every aspect of life. It has been for centuries. The question is, How do we stand in spite of injustice? Some of the biggest minds and noblest lives of centuries past were erased by injustice. What can we do about it? Not much. But we can do a lot about our reaction to it. We can clear our conscience so we would not be the ones committing it. We should always oppose injustice and never side with it. We must remember that those who do the injustice aren't touched by the sorrow of the oppressed. They will just grind their teeth a little more until they find a way to remove all who will portray them as unjust.

Yet, in the most polite way possible, we should uphold truth and honesty and justice and goodness toward all. We must not bend one nanometer toward injuring others. And if we are the ones who are bent by the crooked injustice of others, we should keep standing. We should continue on, developing stamina and persevering in our determination not to consent to injuring others.

Many years ago, my father brought us a boomerang from a visit to Australia. We grabbed it and ran to try the miracle spinning device. But it did not give the expected results. I had to learn how to throw it correctly (which I never did).

The boomerangs that we throw in this life, sooner or later, return to us. If we were throwing them at the innocent, feeling superior, than we too will have to deal with the consequences of that injury one day. It's so interesting to observe how the rules suddenly change when the boomerang returns toward us.

Hand Gestures

To learn one language, I was in a very good private school that offered high-speed, precise, and well-designed classes to ambassadors and businessmen. Upon finishing the class, one ambassador gave us all a visa to visit his country. I never did go, but it was a nice gesture.

I did start to use my "little helper" to better communicate with people—a strategy that was probably designed by the best of the best centuries ago. It works. And it's free. I'm talking about the hands. From the same start. Even after I learned some of the language I was studying, as well as years later when I came to speak it like a parrot, I still was using my hands. And I do so to this day.

I never felt bad about my conversational skills until we moved away and someone called my attention to my hand gesturing. I was a little surprised—a little more than I would like to admit. I remembered growing up in a culture where hands were not used, for example, to demonstrate an airplane propeller. Whether or not to do it was a personal choice. In our household, it was discouraged.

And let's not even mention the Babylon moment of confusion in the brain when you're studying a second or third language and the eyes capture a word that's spelled the same as a word in original language but the brain doesn't have the slightest idea whether it should be pronounced like it is in the original language. You fear being mocked for pronouncing the word wrong. You think that maybe adding a certain amount of twist to the word (sometimes a little letter swallowing helps too) would work and then, hopefully, you'll be understood. There is a third option too. That's to forget all the rest and just focus on twisting. I am not talking about Chubby Checker's song.

Believe it or not, a moment comes when you see the words from the original languages you spoke fluently and the brain wants to add some extra twisting sounds to them just naturally and spontaneously. This is my excuse, but people who've passed through a similar experience will understand it. And it doesn't apply to people who speak just one or two languages. It's easy for them just to learn one more—I guess. The best option is probably the one I chose a long time ago—that's to practice regularly and equally all of the languages you speak. If you're lucky enough to find representatives from all those cultures who speak all of the languages, talk to them. The funniest part is that when you see a word or phrase, translate it with what seems the precise amount of bending, and then nobody comprehends it for they think that a person as educated as you would know how to pronounce the word in its original language.

All that extra thinking process and electrical discharge in our brain for nothing. We should have just said what we saw in the first place. But how do we know when to do it and when not to? So I stand firmly defending my theory about the blessing of using the hands while we're trying to communicate with others—just in the case. One can never be sure. It doesn't cost me a lot to talk about an airplane flight and just nicely lift up my arm to show whomever I'm talking to how the airplane was flying. You never know if you should use the original French word *aéroplane* or the other original and again, of course, French word *avion*. Or you register these original words in the brain but pronounce them ignoring what you saw. And the stars of this critique scenario typically have never experienced the knowledge of more than one language. Isn't it ironic that those who censor the most loudly and with the most negativity are those who really don't have any idea about the subject but like to show their greatness through their censorship? I do believe in a healthy censure and critique. But these stone-throwing people are usually not the most adequate for the job. Stone throwing is never adequate.

Did you realize that, when asked about their positions or professions, people repeat abbreviations? I grew up in a time when titles had their full name and *ay to* us if we wrote a shortened version of anything in important writing. In the last century, everything related to school was important in writing. The only abbreviation I remember being given the choice to use was PS for post scriptum. Now, it's not just a new language. New technology, workplace, and education systems use neo names—all rendered in three letters, which we should supposedly know. I don't. Why all this renaming of jobs we knew from before in simple, no-hands-needed communication where we aren't going to use the new words but shorten them? Couldn't we just cut the original names into three letters? It would be easier. I am not Quintilian. Nor am I Gaius Lucilius, and I am not the first one to use it. But I guess I do have some small tendency to write in a satirical way—sometimes. And this was for sure expressed here. But no more. Back to the standing part and to our hands.

We all have our original language. I'm talking about the language of who we are, of how we express ourselves. Our minds and souls are unique. And we first start thinking that everyone around us is speaking the same language as we are. Then comes the awakening time for some sooner than for others later. The realization enters that we actually do not share the same language with the people around us. The words can appear familiar and we rush to them, but then we realize that they are being pronounced differently. The only thing that was the same was the appearance. And if we try to find that common sense fiber, we can be even mocked. Sometimes we absolutely cannot understand each other, for we were put in unfamiliar surroundings. This could be a new workplace or any new environment. Wherever the place, we feel that the people are speaking Basque, and there is no connection between our language and theirs in the roots or in the interpretation. We can't relate to what's being communicated on any level. We try to use logic, but it doesn't work. Then we go to the twisting and bending part. Sometimes it works, and sometimes it doesn't. We can add the hands too. They are part of us. It gives us some comfort when finally we can be understood.

Some just gave up. They want faster results. Some blend the expected strategies of communicating with their own way of expression. And some strictly follow the cold rule of learning the assigned and nothing else.

All of us want to be comprehended. We all need mutual understanding. Even though people are from different cultures, if they're using pure hand communication, they can understand each other for the needs are the same. We have to use our own hands too. It represents our involvement in life, our striving to understand and to give what we want to share in a unique way of expression. We will not be always understood. Many will ignore our words (I am not talking about the literal words and language but about our ways of expression and life) and not even try to give us time. But we are the ones who have to persevere toward our goal. We must learn from the best sources and, at the same time, rely on our own small inner voice. Many forget their way of speaking for they don't want to be mocked, and they hush all their dreams and wishes. They just focus on the twisting of their own speech, which was unique, in order to become like everyone else around them. They sacrifice their personality. No. It should not happen. Our way of talking is the part of who we are. Always thriving upward and refining the ugly parts, but losing the individual art of expressing ourselves is something we should not permit.

If we see people around us who are not so communicative or just being different, that is not a reason to throw them to the side. It's easy to be with those who make us feel good and glad, but can we sit beside someone who is rejected and try listening to even his or her silence? Maybe this person never uses his or her hands to communicate because he or she was discouraged. Such people never used their own way of expressing who they are. Let's encourage them by using our own hands (our own unique way of being) and bring joy and cheerfulness into their lives. And if they are not so sure how to do it, that's all right. That's why laughter and simple, unaffected nature is here to break the ice. People sense when we act fine and refine and extra fine with them in a plastic way. Nobody needs that. We need to have and give authentic, good-hearted attention to the people around us.

I did look for information, and there was something I didn't ask for. The researchers from serious venues assure us that people who use their hands—get ready—are much more intelligent, warm, agreeable, energetic; the list goes on. I would do it anyway, whether or not Freud and his successors or those who came long before him approved of people using their hands for better communication. It's common sense.

I would never have started to use my hands if I hadn't been brought into the difficult situation of not understanding a word of a foreign language. I grew up in a home where talking with the hands was discouraged entry did as if it were bad manners. So being brought to a situation where I had to communicate with my hands for my survival actually helped me in my way of expressing myself and growing into who I am. Instead of making me insecure, it brought me confidence.

So regardless of situations where nobody will listen or nobody will understand, there is hope. Even when the road seems lonely—for the large group is traveling together, talking, and having a good time, leaving you alone with the excuse of not understanding you—do not give up. Go and learn, keep walking forward, and use your hands. Be yourself. There will be a day when you will encounter people who will start to pay attention to you. And even if this doesn't happen, you won't have sold yourself out for a lesser version of you. You will be very happy that you didn't lose your identity but became a better, more confident, and more secure person. We have to let others express themselves in their unique way too. I am repeating over and over in different packages that we are to be unique—in order to develop our full potential of beauty, love, and kindness and not be cookie-cutter dough that is simply surviving.

Betrayal

"**E**t tu, Brute?"
We know (or not) these famous words that William Shakespeare ascribed to Julius Caesar when he realized that Marcus Brutus, whom he considered his friend, was one of his assassins.

There were actually three people who murdered him on the floor of the Senate–unexpectedly. The assassins of Brutus were not some people from the street. Nor were they open enemies. Decimus was much closer to Caesar than was Brutus, but Shakespeare decided to give more importance to the third one. Decimus was the one who had shown more loyalty to Caesar than the others. Cassius was the one who planned the murder. But it was Decimus who helped Cesar restore his family name and honor. Decimus was not all bad. Oh no. He was a very good soldier, who brought victories for Caesar. Decimus wanted to be recognized. He wanted honors and more power, control, and government. Then there was Gaius Octavius, a possible threat for the position and a good replacement.

The words, "And you, Brutus?" are the words of surprise uttered by Caesar as he realized he was being stabbed by people he thought to be his friends. Or at least he never thought they would be the ones to plot against his life. Through centuries, these words have you been the symbol of betrayal.

Brutus was a common name in that time, and it meant a big, slow, or a stiff-necked animal. The Spanish took over, and the word *bruto* means stupid. I've never heard of somebody naming their child Brutus or Judas, because both are synonyms for betrayal for the lowest of the low. Now if somebody named their children one of these names, it wouldn't mean they love the betrayal. But the symbol is somehow known to be negative. So I do think that people still avoid those names.

Horrors of betrayal are committed through centuries on every level of human existence. And they're always motivated by that unhealthy, dark desire for control, helped by jealousy.

Friedrich Nietzsche tried to define the desire for control and power as a philosophical concept called *der Wille zur Macht* (the will to power). In spite of being tempted, I will not discuss his views here that were used and misused by some ugly regimes in history. We will not solve anything by such a discussion. What is done is done. We have to work with our reality and see how to rise above that suffocating pain of the lowest blow we receive or that somebody we know passed through.

Betrayal comes from those we don't expect to deliver it—from those we trust. It comes from those we opened ourselves up to, expecting this opening to be mutual. Did you notice I did not say a mutual feeling? Oh, the feelings can change and throw us in some strange situations, but we have to be guided by principles—principles that don't fluctuate according to Wall Street. We need principles that ensure we will never go so low as to damage someone's life. Our principles should mean that we treat others like we would like to be treated. The Golden Rule is still the best rule ever. This is the principle of always turning to the truth, like the needle to the pole.

The saying about the wolf in sheep's clothing is as relevant today as it was when it was first said. Traitors like to hide, hiding in sheep's clothing while planning and devising behind the disguise how to destroy. And when they trap their object, the triumph of their victory is manifested by ignoring every plea for mercy.

There is huge damage inside, where the work should be done on perfecting self-control, instead of controlling of others. People who are empty of goodness and nobility try to fill themselves with themselves. And since, after being inflated by themselves, they still feel empty, they have to reach out to control others. Showing that they have power is a priority. And this tops the list of scary things about humanity.

It took me quite a long time to understand why, in the Bible, the cutting of the ear in the case of sudden fear was forgiven but the smooth, planned kiss of betrayal from the so-called friend was condemned. There is a difference between a bad impulsive reaction to something unexpected and the cold, planned, knowing-what-is-being-done action.

If we have the desire of showing control over others in a bad way, it is better that we use that energy to serve. We should just help others, and while we are doing that, we will see the beauty of self-control and service, instead of control and betrayal.

There were two friends, the donkey and the fox. They maintained their friendship for a long time. One day, the two friends went to the woods. Here came the big and scary lion.

The fox, being frightened, jumped to his ingenuity, saying, "I am not afraid of you, big and generous king lion. Would you like the meat of this stupid animal that is with me? I can help you to be served."

The lion accepted the offer, and the fox pushed the donkey friend into the pit.

Then the lion attacked the fox, saying, "I can have the donkey later for he is in the pit. But I will have you now."

If we've betrayed others, let us try to restore as much as possible. And if we were betrayed by others, let us heal the wounds, reaching out to help others, leaving behind the ugliness and reaching toward beauty. There is a lot of truth in these words of Oscar Wilde:

> Yet each man kills the thing he loves
> By each let this be heard
> Some do it with a bitter look
> Some with a flattering word
> The coward does it with a kiss
> The brave man with a sword.

Let us not betray but be faithful and firm like the rock to do always good.

The Tunnels

I love the plain highways where I live, and I do not miss the tunnels. I didn't drive through long tunnels for years, and I am very grateful for that sunlight experience while driving. Beautiful scenery of almost nothing in the desert is better than a tunnel. (This does not have to be a shared opinion.)

I remember as a child riding on a train, and we did try them all. We rode the diesel train, the old-fashioned steam train, and the fast ICE that was a recently new thing back then. It can travel at the speed of 320 kilometers per hour.

Just imagine that speed and all the old-fashioned obstacles on the road, like mountains for example. Back there in Europe, they do have tunnels and some more tunnels. It seems to me that they are building some more again. The longest tunnel is there too—at just fifty-seven kilometers long. There are enough of them; in order to get to our destinations faster, they have to make some new holes under the mountains. Maybe we could still go around the mountains and watch the scenery in the trains that were actually not so slow, but we want to go faster in flashier styles of travel. Then the price has to be paid so we can invest in new ways to get there.

In my time, not all the tunnels had lights. Actually, in my memory, no tunnels had any light at all. Inside them was pure concentrated darkness. Yes, some did have lights but not the tunnels for the rail. I didn't know if I preferred passing through them in the car or by train. Either of the choices was scary.

Remember the old saying *to see the light at the end of the tunnel*? It refers to someone being deep down in some problem or trial and waiting to come out of it. So, please, do not go into every detail of the modern achievement of tunnel construction, comparing it to what I'm saying. I am just using an old metaphor. A tunnel is a symbol of uncertainty and dark trials and not seeing the hope ahead.

There was one tunnel in Austria that simply had the ability to bring out in me every fear possible. It was so long that you could compose a new addition to the Strauss waltzes while driving through—if the fear wasn't there. Some sense of solemnity just overtook the air. We would try to count or to sing or to talk, pretending everything was just fine, but it didn't work. It is a truth that, in the company of others, it wasn't so bad. But still, every second counted.

Maybe you would laugh at that, but we were hearing the news. Every now and then we heard about an accident—in the tunnel. Or some of the accidents were on the railroad, but in my head, it was all classified in the same group.

Just think about that for a moment. If you enter a tunnel, there is no change of opinion, no repentance, no U-turn, and no possibility of returning. There is an entrance and an exit and nothing between. So if you enter, the only possibility is to come out on the other side. You have to move forward, not backward. Why did you enter? Because everybody was entering that way or because you wanted to get somewhere faster. But this is no longer the question to be answered once you're inside.

If you are driving, the answer is to focus on the road and drive. Look for that tiny point that indicates the entrance back into the normal world. I know that the tunnels are not so dark anymore, and people currently are glued to their technological devices (in or out the tunnel). So for the majority, traveling through tunnels is no longer a big deal. Some even love tunnels. However, we get special safety advice for driving through tunnels for there is a real difference between driving along the road in the country and driving in a deep dark hole.

One piece of advice is to check your fuel. Some tunnels are really long. And in the middle of a tunnel is not the time to discover that there is no fuel. With all the devices, technology, lights, and modernization, the car will still not go without the fuel.

The majority of cars automatically turn on the headlights, but some don't. If driving in one of those that don't, you have to be sure to switch your headlights on and be sure they're on low beam so you don't blind the people coming from the opposite side and you can see where are you driving.

Believe it or not, you have to take off your sunglasses. Maybe you had them to protect your eyes from the sun or to hide behind them or because of a headache or just to show off the latest fashion. It doesn't matter anymore. Sunglasses have no practical and no esthetical use in the tunnel. There is no sunshine thereunder.

Keep a distance from the vehicle in front of you. Observe the speed limit—the maximum as well as the minimum. And, yes, congestion can happen inside also. Your cell phone will probably not have a signal there, so you might just not be able to speak to anyone while waiting.

Why did we end up in a tunnel of life? Maybe we were rushing to get the most out of life and did not want to take some other road that would take us more time. We avoided roads with more scenery to watch while driving, where we could think and decide about our destination with more than just a moment. We choose the fastest route. Could it be that we were just caught in the moment and followed the crowd? Or did we simply follow our instincts, not calculating the price? Or perhaps we were faithfully following the map yet ended up in the tunnel—for life is ironically nondiscriminatory when it comes to disappointments and hurt, pain and sorrow.

You can be from the times of the Train Eclair de luxe or from a time when you never saw anything but high-speed trains. Perhaps you prefer to travel in first class, where you are provided more comfort and facilities. Or you might be just as fine in second class. The train of life will probably take you through tunnels that can be short or can last miles and miles, and you'll be wondering if you will ever see the light.

Society told us not to care for we can just amuse ourselves with our devices and ignore reality. So some got used to spending years and years of their lives in some mind-numbing activities, sitting on the carousel and wasting their potential. The tunnel became normal for them. They had no need for seeing the light at the end for they didn't miss it anymore. This became a comfortable place for them.

By driving your own car, you have more options to choose from. But you may still end up in some tunnel. Take off your sunglasses and just be you. You need to see the road clearly. You need to follow that beam of light in front of you. If you have good lights on your car and think you've figured out how to get to the end safely, don't be too proud about that. Don't shine your bright lights on the vehicles traveling in the opposite direction. That extra strong light shining in their faces can make it hard for them to focus. Just focus on your lane and use your vehicle's low beam to light your way.

Don't give people your opinions that are too shiny for them at this moment of their lives. You are still in the tunnel, just like they are. And having better lights does not make you the better ubication than them.

We should not drive over the speed limit. That can be very dangerous. But driving too slowly is just as bad. We might focus so much on our own troubles that we block other people's lives. We are not the only ones passing through troubles. There are many more around us, and while helping them, we are moving forward. While thinking about others, we are advancing. While we think of how to improve and become better than we were before entering the darkness, we are focusing on the road. While we are trying to see that light at the end of the tunnel, we are growing hope. And while we are focusing on our own improvement, the rear lights of our vehicle will ease the way for someone behind us.

Rough Waters

After my son was born, we traveled a lot by ship. I detested those giants. Just staring at them made me dizzy. And I was still standing on solid ground. So I would just enter the cabin and try to go to sleep, hoping that morning would come very soon. Somehow during daylight, the struggles seemed a little more bearable. For some people, those journeys on the ship were the high point of their lives. They enjoyed the food and music and whatever was there. But for me, this was a mere minute-counting occasion. And those minutes were passing very slowly— not to mention the hours.

Then one day, we switched for an even bigger ship and better cabins. But still, I remained miserable, seasick, and scared. Every time. I would arrive at our destination exhausted. Don't get me wrong. I had traveled on ships and boats before. But I'd been on familiar waters, where one can almost see the coast or some island. I'd felt safe and at home. That was along the Adriatic coast, which is the northernmost arm of the Mediterranean Sea. But here I was in the deep, cold water of the ocean, and I was scared.

Then one day, I do not remember anymore how, the captain of the ship invited us to have dinner with him. I guess somebody had told him about us for he was from Greece. The ship belonged to the same country too but sailed under a different flag. He sent for us to move into the best cabin on the ship, and we had the best care possible. Following that, every time we traveled, the crew would let us have our special privileges, and one of which was that we could be on the bridge all we wanted. My son especially enjoyed it. I never believed in abusing the kindness, so we didn't stay in these special accommodationz alll the time. The calm and very confident posture and behavior of the captain made all of us more secure too. Just knowing the captain makes a person more confident, and the fear somehow vaporizes. After all, he was from the land of the best ship business-knowing people. I guess all of us thought that Onassis converted everyone into a shipping expert in Greece. Of course, they were experts for centuries but Onassis added even more to our assurance.

One day, I noticed the glass open-air wing extensions on the sides of the bridge. My son was there with the captain looking for the pilot's arrival. I would not stand on that glass-floored box for anything in this world. There they were, looking for a brave pilot in a small boat traveling through the rough waters to get close and then climb on the ship while it was moving—a simply amazing feat. If I hadn't been on the bridge, I would never have known about the importance of maritime pilots. I always thought the captain was the entire brain and heart of the vessel. But I was wrong. Thankfully I learned. Sometimes the invisible, the behind-the-scenes, the unapplauded and unrecognized is equally important, if not more than the insignias we see. We should recognize all.

William J. H. Boetcker said years ago that a man without religion or spiritual vision is like a captain who finds himself in the midst of an uncharted sea, without compass, rudder, and steering wheel. He never knows where he is, which way he is going, or where he is going to land.

How sad it is to see so many of our lives mirroring that description. Some of us are being tossed by waves here and there while having music and dance and food and entertainment. Others are just feeling miserable, counting minutes for days to pass. Then we justify everything with the famous quote that we are the captains of our own lives. This is essentially the truth, but we do need a pilot too—if we plan to enter that harbor safely.

The captain is the brain of the ship, but the pilot is the brain of the waters he knows very well. The two have to communicate well and work together. In the case of stubbornness on one or both sides, the ship could finish in a wreck. Thankfully, that is not usually the case. How many shipwrecks in the rough waters of our lives, instead of the peaceful sailing and entrance into the harbor, result from lack of good correlation and collaboration?

The pilot is responsible for maneuvering the ship through the dangerous waters and bringing them all safely into the harbor. He's from the local area, so he isn't on the ship all the time. He has to take a special boat close to the ship and enter through a little opening on that colossal steel wall. And during this process the waters can be calm or not so calm. It can be very windy and the waves rough, yet the pilot has to come on board and help the captain conduct the ship safely to its destiny.

Who is our pilot who helps us navigate safely and securely through the rough waters of this life? Do we just arrive at whatever harbor at the peril of entering by ourselves or do we have some charts and a compass? Is there a north on our compass, something fixed and sure that gives us security and a point of reference? Can we stand still in the midst of the windy ocean, as we know the captain as well as the pilot?

If we do, we can sleep safely for the fear will be gone. We'll know that our lives are in safe and responsible hands that are working out the best for us.

The Wind

Hurricanes are big and come and go, but winds can blow for a long time. They can blow for days or even longer. They can be, at first, very interesting, like the kind of wind that let's us fly kites. But after a while, especially if the winds intensify and are accompanied by the rain, there is not too much charm left. There can be some windy people in our lives—people who we think flying kites with is nice. Or maybe we are the windy ones. But after a while, it becomes draining. We can drain all the energy from ourselves and others too with our moving of the air.

Being a small child, I did not like September when school started. None of us did. The nice summer days were passing away, and fall was coming. Little by little, the days grew colder and colder. Then came the season of rubber boots and raincoats—every day. And the wind was sometimes so strong that it made our umbrellas fly away and other items too, like hats. It's good that it didn't take us also. Sometimes we got together and pushed against the wind. Sometimes we just closed our eyes and peeked out through our eyelashes toward the road, while at the same time hanging tightly to our hats.

We need some wind in our lives. There's nothing more calming than a smooth breeze under the sunny day. I did live in the tropics, and I can assure you that we do need a nice breeze. We need sun and rain, as well as breeze and calm. But when one element is predominant and goes beyond the limit, then the situation is not so inviting.

Wind is not pleasant at all, but since it can't be changed, it can be used for our good. Columbus was very glad when the needed wind started to blow, and taking off into the wind allows pilots to achieve a higher altitude in less time and with less speed. Wind blowing on a small seedling or newly emerged spring plant helps it create a stronger stem. Each time a plant is pushed by the wind, it releases a hormone called an auxin that stimulates the growth of supporting cells. What would Holland do without the wind? And what about the many other farmers around the world who used wind energy for their needs?

Sometimes we can't change the winds around us, but surely we can convert them into very good help. Some of them will even help us take off easier and reach new heights or develop a stronger stem.

There was a story about the sun and the wind. They were arguing over who is stronger. A man bellow was walking in the cold autumn day. The wind said, boasting, "Let's test the question on him. We'll find out who is stronger, you or me. You'll see when I get to him, he will lose his coat immediately."

The sun agreed.

The wind wanted to show off, so he started first. He blew stronger and stronger, and the more he did, more tightly the traveler below held onto his coat. He would curse the wind, but he wouldn't let go of his coat or hat.

The sun, seeing the deficiency of the wind, came out and started sending its rays to the ground to dry it. The air became warmer and the traveler bellow took off his coat and his hat and continued to walk.

"You see," said the sun to the wind, "more can be done by goodness and mercy than with roughness."

The Dutch people did not just create windmills, they converted many more disadvantages and unfavorable circumstances into a real blessing. For me, their land is a symbol of taking the negative, the unjust, the windy, and the less fortunate and transforming it into something beautiful, into a blessing, into an advantage. It required hard and determined work to build dikes and create polders and to take the negative and convert it into magnificent fields of tulips. Tulips didn't originate in Holland, but it was the Dutch who converted them into one of their biggest hallmarks and industries. To get a beautiful tulip requires hard work. And the bigger the challenge, the more abundant will be the rejoicing upon seeing the positive outcome.

If the winds have long been blowing in our path, and we are drained and tired of holding onto our hats and umbrellas and of not seeing life normally but only peeking through our eyelashes, it's time to stop. It's time to stop losing energy against the wind for it is too strong for us. We should work on regaining the land from the sea around us and start to build our own windmills. While working the soil, we must put some bulbs into it.

Though we won't see any changes in the beginning, this is when the bulbs are slowly extending their roots under the ground. Very soon, we will have fields of the most beautiful tulips. The colors may vary according to our personal taste. Let's take the disadvantage of the wind and convert it into fuel for our advantage.

The Cold

I do like to remember my snow experience from childhood like it was—cold. We did not go out just to play. We also had to walk to school and back. I'm realizing now that the adults had to do their daily duties in the harshness of the winter or under the burning sun. We children were protected from that reality. And yes, we loved to go out to play. My parents would always find a time for us to make a snowman, to go sleigh riding, or to make the best figures by falling into a deep snow. (No, we did not call them snow angels.) But the time of coming into the house, where there were no scientific speculations about the ideal temperature on the thermostat, was my favorite part.

It was warm and cozy. And nothing, absolutely nothing can compare to the good old-fashioned, all-from-scratch cooking of our mothers. They knew how to cook well every day. To sit at the table with red defrosted cheeks and hungry tummies was such a great time. Our noses were in the thawing stage too. The cold and good laughter outside ensured none of us were short of appetite.

My father had to stay up late at night to finish his work he brought home, recompensing the time we played outside. But he never underlined that for us. He never claimed his goodness toward us for sacrifices like that. Looking back and having my own children, I am amazed. How did we become so selfish in today's world? But that is another subject entirely. We have to go back to the cold.

All the wonderful snow memories aside, I still loved the warm weather. And you can't blame me for dreaming about *Blue Hawaii*. I loved the summers on the Adriatic coast. My favorite summers were the ones we shared with our friends on the southern side of the coast. I'm wondering if it's possible that we thought that lying down in that sun for hours, like sardines on the beach was actually the glorious time of our lives. It had to be a consequence of some minor heat stroke directly to the brain.

Don't get me wrong. I don't like the cold, but I'm no fan of the equatorial sun's rays shining directly on me. I did get under the equatorial sun too for years. I'm grateful for the sun and the snow, but nothing in its extreme is ideal. I guess this is some sign of aging, where wisdom tries to teach us some lessons.

I am grateful for every invention that can change the cold to warmth and the heat into a breathable experience. Now, what I know for sure is that, through centuries, people would not be as afraid of the hot weather as they were of the cold. There was always a fire to heat up the cold, but no air-conditioning system was invented before 1902! And if you didn't have some ostrich feathers and, in the best case, someone to blow it toward you, the chance is you had to endure the heat of the day.

As for all of you who love the cold outside, I am glad for you. I love it also, if I watch it through the window or at least am guaranteed that, after a good time spent outside, I can be in a warm cozy home without the thermostat cookie-cutting theory about the perfect temperature. I am going with the good old-fashion way of a warm fire that is there not for the purpose of aesthetic or romantic feeling but to warm us up. Aesthetics and romance can be added under the bonus category.

One early morning a couple of years ago, I heard a strange noise. It sounded like something was breaking outside. I ran toward the window and looked outside just in time to see the tree in front of our house splitting in half—just like that. Then there was another sound just like the first one; another tree just fell to the ground, followed by another and another. We lived surrounded by plenty of trees, and they were falling to the ground—one by one. By the full morning, every tree on our long driveway was destroyed. The trunks of some trees were halved, some came out completely, and some lost their crowns.

I was just taking pictures and sending them to everyone, as what I was witnessing was completely unbelievable. I learned that it was an ice storm. As with every intense storm, the story doesn't end there. Consequences are the worst in every intense storm—the effects after the storm.

There was no electricity for weeks. Gratefully, we had running water, but many didn't. Seeing yesterday's beautiful trees, the symbol of greatness and strength, ripped away, losing their crowns and glory was shocking. They started to fall just like that—no warning signs.

Suddenly things changed from questions of pleasure and taste to mere survival and hope for just the electricity—just a current that brings life into the house.

Human coldness can be like that. It has the ability to make us mere survivors, expecting some current of a better life or some good news of hope. Coldness can cut and split and not care about its effects at all— breaking down our crowns and leaving us with just a bare trunk. Asking coldness for compassion is impossible.

Trying to hang the branches back in place will not repair the broken tree. It could be done, but after a while, it will be clear that the fallen branch is getting dry and is no longer part of the tree. Some of us tried to glue back the broken branches, but with time, the truth became visible. It was not the tree like it should be. It did not belong together anymore.

So as with every chapter in *Still Standing in Spite of*, the message is the same. We have to stand up and put up some extra clothing on, because it is cold. And we have to start removing the fallen branches. We must cut them and clean up the area. While we do that, the current of light will come back too. The cut trunks and branches can be used as fuel to heat us up with good old fire. So too can the pieces we cut away be our fuel, giving us the strength to be warmed up and live life again. Their warmth can enable us to go forward, appreciating every blessing we have in our daily life, even if it is a simple ostrich feather.

The update on the trees is that the first spring after the storm was depressing and odd. But the trees did their best to bloom again the next year. And the year after that, some new branches grew on them. Lately, we don't even compare the old trees with these new heroes of survival. They made up for what was lost and worked on the parts that were left. They have the most beautiful foliage. I am sure that, if we would examine the trees, we would find some scars. But why focus on that? The trees put all their energy toward restoration and regeneration—just like we can.

Artificiality

I feel very fortunate to have learned how to cook when I was just a child. It wasn't just me. All the kids around me knew the basics. When I say "cook," in my mind I still see a sack of flour, some water, sometimes yeast, salt, and perhaps oil, along with whatever extra basic ingredients were in season. The basic ingredients came from our garden or the marketplace. I see an apron, clean hands, and no cookbooks of any kind. What you cooked was a natural thought process that occurred as you were gathering the ingredients.

From the same basic ingredients, you could create dozens and dozens of different types of food every day. You could make your own plain pasta or ravioli or perhaps some kind of flatbread or pita bread with homemade falafel. What if you decided you preferred a pizza or maybe a calzone? What about strudels or just spanakopita? The ideas are endless. With the same flour, we could make pastries or just a loaf of bread.

If you really know the basics of cooking, all the rest is just improvising. You can't leave out the main ingredients, but all the others can be replaced or the recipe modified. You become naturally creative. All of us use the same basic ingredients for the same kind of food. Yet each household has its special taste and special way of making it. They add their personal touch.

However, we are being bombarded every day at each step by the fast food industry. On offer is, of course, fast, highly seasoned food with added flavor enhancers, altered in laboratories, shaped into the "perfect" shape and size with machines, and available twenty-four hours a day seven days a week, just a minute away. Society around us has gotten used to that, and there is no way that the time-consuming, hardworking, old-fashioned food creation from our kitchens can compete with it. It without a doubt cannot compete with fast food's perfectness in shape. Nor can it match the perfectly calculated timing for serving.

When we were children and smelled the unique aroma from the kitchen, we would ask when the food would be done. The answer was given not in minutes and seconds but usually longer.

I must confess I gave in too—sometimes. I would choose, at those times, foods that were closest possible to their natural source, but they were still processed—a little bit here and there and then more and more. It's just so much easier. I am grateful for the ways and means of making things not difficult. I am no longer preparing artery-clogging rich cakes or pastries, for they are time-consuming and, at the same time, taxing our health. I am in a stage of my life where I want to consciously take care of my body and not be irresponsible with my health. I am very thankful that I could learn from others from so many different cultures and take the best from everyone. And I did simplify many things. Yet the idea of having food ready in minutes is just so tempting.

So apparently, homemade meals are losing against their perfect imitation. But there is something. The core of everything is in the taste. The imitation does not even come close to the real authentic taste of a homemade meal. That's why good restaurants cost more. Preparing healthy food from scratch requires much more time and effort, as does finding and harvesting quality ingredients.

The only things on the homemade side of the food balance scale are taste and personal satisfaction. Everything else is on the other side— appearance, convenience, shape and size, together with instant satisfaction.

I know there are people who work hard every day outside the home and just want to come home and relax. I do understand that. So they consume what is easier for them. I am talking here about the principle, not a sole action of eating or not eating homemade food.

But if you ask me what I prefer, my answer will always be homemade food—made with authentic ingredients and prepared with care.

With the same basic ingredients of love and kindness, hard work and honesty, and compassion and grace, we can do so much good. It will take more labor, time, effort and determination, but we can bring a new taste to the people around us—a joyful taste. We can approach people on a person-to-person basis, more spontaneously and not so perfectly artificial. We can go out and do good from the heart, adjusting the ingredients according to people's needs.

Perhaps they will not appreciate the approach, for their taste buds are accustomed to imitation and to the artificial. But having patience and giving them time could bring some changes. Maybe after a while, they will realize the value of the true taste.

Vengeance and Revenge

The older I get, the more and more I appreciate the school I attended during my elementary school years. Considered by today's standards, it was ultrastrict. The material we had to learn and the skills we were expected to know surpass what many students even in high school are required to master today. May I add even in colleges? Would I go back to that school? I'm not so sure. But I am grateful for every step of my journey.

Physical education was very important in those countries in those times. The words "I can't" had no significance. It seemed to me that we had to do exercises every day. And I am talking hard-core, preparing-for-the-Olympics, no-mercy-style workouts.

We had to go through every movement in world-denominated sport. The only deviation from the path was dance class—a strict dance class. That was the shortest course of all, as the emphasis was on the gymnastics. I still remember the winter of my fourth grade. It was very cold, with snow piled high outside, and the physical education teacher decided it was time we learn to get outside and run for forty-five minutes around the gym building. We thought that we would have the gymnastic classes inside, so we had just our tiny outfits for that.

Nobody died, and we all survived. Actually, we started to do this on a regular basis. One day outside in cold weather, one day in the gym. Our gyms did have very good heating, so we got used to our strengthening training.

I don't know how much you know about gymnastics. Maybe you've watched it during the Olympic games. The basics in this exercises is to have perfect balance, flexibility as if there are no bones inside in you, the strength of steel, and an equally impressive level of endurance. It does not come overnight. Mastering gymnastics requires hours and hours of hard work and self-discipline. It also develops mental alertness and self-confidence.

And then came the day I will never forget. Before every class started, we had to stand in the line by height. I was always closer to the beginning. So I could not hide behind the others. We had to stand in line and turn toward the vault. The vault is like a pommel horse but without handles. In vaulting events, gymnasts sprint down a 25-meter runway, jump onto a springboard (or perform a round-off or handspring entry onto a springboard), land momentarily inverted on the hands on the vaulting horse or vaulting table (preflight segment), and then propel themselves forward or backward off that platform to a two-footed landing (postflight segment).

I had to google this to get the correct definition in English for I never thought about gymnastics in any other language than the one I was using during my school days. I never dreamed of reconnecting with gymnastics.

Now, if you'll notice, we did fly. The terms here—*preflight* and *postflight*—refer to taking off and landing. Fortunately, there were no passengers. For some of us did land badly. That was not, however, a problem for our teacher. He would send us back to the line. Every time, it seemed farther and farther back. Some would get to the springboard and just stop. It looked so terrible. Impossible. Some would jump on the springboard but just stay on it. Our teacher did not care.

One day, I started to hear a noise in my ears. Everything started spinning around me. I didn't have strength anymore. I knew I would just collapse. I felt cold sweat and barely walked to my teacher, saying that I just couldn't do it. He sent me back to the line. The class time had ended a long time ago, but he was determined. All around the gym were the bleachers, on which sat the next group, waiting its turn. They watched us, the small people, in our struggle. Some mocked. Others encouraged. I didn't even care about them. I just came to the point where I determined that I was going to take off and fly and then land with my two feet one beside each other.

I ran. I gave my last joule of energy and determination, and then I heard the cheering. I did it. I think the stronger ones helped us weaker ones to survive the rest of the day.

Is it too much to say that, in spite of all of the sweat and pain and discouragement and faint, I felt good that I had done it? Can I add that I actually liked the vault after that and would perform on it on my own?

Needless to say, the next day we had another class preparing us for expertise on the balance beam. Was it easier than the vault? The vault looked like child's play compared to this.

If you think that a beam more than a meter in height, just ten centimeters wide, and about five meters long is a fun place to jump and do somersaults following someone's choreography, believe me, it is not. You have a little more than a minute to perform all you are expected to do. And if you are scared, they will answer that there is a blue padded mattress at the end of the beam. How do you get there if you are falling from the middle of the beam? I never found an answer. One thing I did know was this—you should never focus on the floor, where you could eventually fall.

What to do when you are wronged? The very first thought, the initial impulse is to return bad for bad or just to make things even. Perhaps, we feel a desire to get what we lawfully deserve to have. Whatever the reasoning, everything in us cries for revenge. How bad is to see people walk over you and not even blink in the process? What to do? Should we leave the case and simply focus on our own path? Or should we prove that we are right? Should we stand up and walk away from the epicenter of the evil and try to build up our own lives, not spending time planning vengeance?

That sounds easy on paper. Similarly, it was easy for the teacher to send us back. But in real life it causes a real struggle. I know that for sure!

When all the voices that are loving and caring are telling us to ask for our rights, when our own mind reasons with us that injustice is a good reason for revenge, what then? Do we listen to our reasoning that says it's impossible to jump off a springboard do a somersault, followed by a complete turnaround, and land on our two feet?

Or do we try again and again against our nature, against provocation from injustice, and against our own feeble human frame that feels it is too much, until we jump, turn over our lives toward something better, and then nail a good landing on the landing pad on the other side? There we will find a new side, a new way of seeing things. There, we will become fully aware of the beauty of this new achievement, which we thought impossible to accomplish.

After that experience, we come to realize that revenge is cheap. It does not require resistance. But to stand still in spite of injustice and not return evil with evil takes extra perseverance, extra balance, and extra mental ability. And doing so contributes to our development in every aspect of our lives. It develops flexibility that few can have. We come to see the world from a higher level for we can walk on a beam that is elevated above the ground, not looking at the place where we could fall but focusing ahead.

Foolishness

There is an old story that tells how, in the city of Constantinople, there lived an old drunkard whose father left him a huge treasure of inheritance but who lost it all and now had only a blanket and an old hat that was falling apart. One day, the king was walking on the street. Seeing the man, the king started scolding him for losing all that inheritance and becoming what he had become.

"It is my thing if I am drinking. And I'm doing it with my own money," the drunkard replied. "And if you think I do not have money, for how much will you sell me half of the city?"

The king knew that the man didn't have any money but suspected that somebody could give it to him if he agreed. So he gave an amount and said. "I will sell you half of the city for this amount so both of us can rule the city. Bring me the money tomorrow."

When the morning came and the drunkard realized what foolishness he had done, he did not appear in front of the king. The king sent for him and heard the confession that he didn't have the money. Outraged, the king ordered his execution.

But the drunkard pleaded for life, saying, "Do whatever you want to, but first find a blind man in the city who does not see at all and a man who does not have legs and a man who is so poor that he doesn't have anything in this world. See what you will learn from them."

The king was intrigued by this strange request and did what was asked. The blind man, the man without legs, and the poor man were served the king's food. After they ate and drank, the blind man said, "Thank you, king, for the white bread and the red wine. That was such a feast."

"How do you know it was white bread and red wine if you cannot see? I will kick you right now," yelled the man without the legs.

And the poor one exclaimed, "Do it for me too, and I will pay you."

"Do you see now, king, what the drink is doing?" the old man said. "It causes the blind to see, the lame to walk, and the poor to have money. That is how I had enough money yesterday to pay you for half of the city."

The king was sorry for the old man and spared his life.

In the evening, the king, still wondering at the amazing power of the wine, asked to try some. In the morning, he had such a headache that nobody could help him. He ordered his servants to bring the drunkard for he only could help.

When the drunkard came, the king asked what to do for the headache.

The man replied, "Drink the same thing you did last night, and the pain will immediately disappear."

"But then what after tomorrow morning when the headache comes again?" asked the king.

"You drink again and again until you are left like me, with nothing but a blanket."

Human foolishness can be a tricky subject. For none of us is perfectly wise. Moliere said a long time ago that a learned fool is more a fool than an ignorant fool. There are people who, like the man from the story, know that they are doing foolishness but just do not see a way to stop doing it. And they perhaps recognize that they did act unwisely, but they need a helping hand and some extra patience. Some of us—better said, all of—us have committed some foolishness along the path. Maybe we still do.

But then there are those who Moliere mentions who know all the ways and excuses of doing wrong things and will not yield to any common sense. Sometimes, the best way to learn is to go through the consequence of our own actions. Sometimes that can be too much and some compassionate and wise hand can help us make the right decision. Maybe we could be that hand to someone. The tools are wisdom and compassion, not the atomic-resolution holography electron microscope. That is, we can help in the cases when the person is willing to take our help. If not, he or she has to be left to his or her foolishness. We all must have our own time and pace.

We have to braid a strong rope of wise people around us and learn ways that are higher than common foolishness and restore the time we wasted. And we should be merciful, knowing that we could commit some foolishness too due to a headache.

Hope That Is Gone

Lily of the valley—I have not smelled this flower in decades, but its fragrance is still alive in my memory. The lily of the valley was the first flower we saw after the winter. Actually, while we still had snow, it was the snowdrop. And then came the violets, which we went to pick in the fields. But in my mind, the impact of the beauty and excitement after the winter is found in the lily of the valley.

My grandmother had these flowering plants around the fence, and we could find them around some other houses and fields too. They filled the air all around with their sweet, unique scent. There is nothing fancy or deluxe about the flower. It's not impressive in size or shape. Its uniqueness, alongside the smell, lies in its simple yet delicate flowers that are in the shape of little bells.

I love tulips in their majestic simplicity too. They are so lofty yet so simple. I remember staring inside the flowers while sitting on the ground— as if such profundity could be found within them. I recall, too, the hyacinth, with its distinctive pleasant aroma that I loved to smell again and again. But nothing replaces the little white flowers with their simple gracefulness.

In the times prior to my grandparents' time, young ladies and young men would pick the lilies of the valley, believing it would bring them happiness and love. And it was the symbol of the returning happiness and pure heart after the long winter days.

There are some products claiming they smell like the lily of the valley, but they aren't even close. Nothing can compare to the natural, to the simple, to the genuine, to the delicate.

The winter days can be long and gray, cold and lonely. Everything around us seems bleak and harsh. This can put us into a state of serious discouragement and make us feel miserable. Some, seeing the time that flew away, lose hope. Some just settle for peace today but deep inside know they could choose another path. The gray penetrates every aspect of our lives and brings its heaviness. Some are filled with deep melancholy and some with regrets. Some feel abandoned and betrayed. Some long for new life but do not know where or how to start. Some are weighed down by fears of all kinds, fears whose ugly shadows are enlarged in the winter light. Some ache in pain that nobody knows about.

Many of us can enjoy having a good time in company and association. We are feasting while cracking nuts and drinking homemade apple cider. But there are people around us who are lonesome and without hope. Our not being in the winter of our lives doesn't mean that is true for everyone.

For all who have had to go through long, lonely, and cold winter days, we should be the lily of the valley. We should bring the hope of returning happiness. The crowd will never understand the heartrending agony of trials that make our lives a winter—bleak and hopeless. They may not appreciate the spring so much or the delicacy of the flowers. For they never had to go through excruciating pain, praying for some ray of hope. That's why, for us, spring is so pleasant—we had to walk in the sorrow of the winter. And we enjoy it fully, while others cannot explain why.

We can't be the imitation of hope and happiness, for the fake will not even come close to the genuine. Just realizing the fact that it works and wanting to impress others is not the best initiator. We have to be the message. It has to become our nature—if we want to be that fragrance of hope.

Let's, with simple gracefulness, announce to the hopeless that the winter is but for a season. Let our perfume fill the air with love and hope. Let those who are without hope receive the aroma and lift their weary heads and hearts. Let the young and the old become cheerful because we announced to them that there are new expectations, new achievements, and new aspirations they can start to follow. We can be the small flower in their spring, infusing them with thoughts to dare to dream again, to look at the sun, and to "renew their strength."

Like always, there will be those who just do not understand the fine fibers of the human heart, those who do not care about others and are only out for themselves. They are living in their summers, purposely ignoring the fact that, one day, winter will knock on their door also. There are those who go around stepping on the precious delicate flowers and crushing them.

But the elevated nature of the simple little flowers is that, even when they are crushed, broken, and bruised by the heavy step of the foe, their last act is to release their beautiful, sweet fragrance. In doing so, they announce, even more clearly, the hope of returning happiness and love.

Different Surroundings

Galileo was another wise man who believed that we can always learn something from others and that the authority of a thousand is not worth the humble reasoning of a single individual. He was referring to the field of science, but we can apply it to our daily lives also.

Looking back, I am very grateful for the rich learning experiences I've had at every stepping-stone of life. Sometimes I've been pushed into a process of assimilation, sometimes I've voluntarily accepted it, and sometimes it was a long spontaneous process of slow learning. Now there were times of pure resistance too. Why would I learn something from someone I considered, sadly, inferior? But thanks to mercy and undeserved grace, we can open our eyes and see more clearly that we are not superior or inferior. All of us have something precious to share with others. What we have is maybe precious to us and not relevant to others, but it is the best we can offer—at the moment.

I have lived in different cultures and traveled with my parents, and I loved to see different ways of living, until it did not have to become a way of life. I was very careful not to lose my own traditional way of living, almost considering it a sacrilege to accept something new from other cultures.

But because of the location of our home, people loved to come there, and we loved to share. We would share over food. What better way is there?

There was some piano playing and singing too, and some heavy topics were discussed. You would think that we were in the Agora of Athens. This built many bridges. People from Argentina to Boston felt at home visiting. I learned that every South American country has its own flavor and customs. We would learn how to make different dishes from each of those countries. You can eat empanada from Argentina, empanada from

Venezuela, empanada from any other South American country—and all of them are different.

I still remember my precious friend who taught me about the matchless Cuban sandwich. It was the best. Mexican tamales and Puerto Rican *pasteles* are not the same. Finally, I gave in and started using cilantro. I don't know how that affected humankind, but for me, it was a giant leap.

Am I trying to tell you all the different ways of making rice and beans? No. Did I mention that, in every Spanish-speaking country the words do not mean the same? It can be *choclo* or *maíz* for the same corn, *durazno* or *melocotón* for the peach. And we are still talking Spanish.

I am a strong believer that until somebody understands the cuisine of a particular people and the way to prepare it, he or she cannot understand the culture completely. A person can live in a place for ages and even learn the language, but there is something about gathering and preparing food together.

Our visitors would call each other names based on their skin color, and nobody got offended. There was not this artificially imposed ethical correctness along every step of the way. Rather, there was a nice, relaxed, and spontaneous—and at the same time, polite—way of building bridges.

How can be that translated to our standing?

When we are surrounded by different people who do not think like us or share the same convictions we have, it can be difficult. But let's try to find a way to get to them. We should do so never ever lowering our standards but understanding that, even though we speak the same language, we can still use other words. This means that we cannot put all in the same sack and just label them. Let's learn to see in every individual the beauty that is typical for him or her.

And perhaps we can put aside our traditional dishes and learn some new ones too. The way we see things can be correct, but it doesn't mean we can't add something to it or cut something out of it.

We can enrich our lives by learning from the aged; from the young; from the abandoned; from the learned, and from the blue, black, pink, yellow, red, white, green, or whatever color we are. People should be valued by the color of their hearts, not by the skin.

Impulsivity

There are people who like to drive and listen to some kind of noise. Some folks like to hear music or just to talk. A few listen to the spoken subject of their interest. Certain people prefer absolute silence, as I do when driving through unknown places or on roads with heavy traffic. I am realizing that it is not just about how we are driving; we have to think for others too. Many times, the people around us drive by impulse, not following the basic guidance that provides a safer driving time for all.

One night, I was driving home and a car in front of me doubled the dose of the red on its rear lights, so suddenly I had to press my brake pedal too with all my might. Before I continue, I will add that I really miss the old times when the rear lights on cars were clearly divided by their function in three simple colors—colors that, even without staring at the back of the car in front of us, called our attention with its bright yellow signal, for example. That particular night, the driver ahead did not even bother to use a signal to indicate that he or she would be turning left, on the higher-than-average speed limit road, across a double yellow line. But right there, after this abrupt breaking, the driver decided to turn his or her vehicle one hundred and eighty degrees. I didn't have time to be too concerned with all the bags in my car that flew to the floor or the danger for the cars coming in the opposite direction. I didn't have time to think about the cars behind me. My *bouquet de fleurs was* smashed also.

Thankfully, I was following the car in front of me with enough distance between us so the only damages were the smashed bags and an almost short circuit of my heart's electrical system. Or simply said, my heart was beating rapidly—so rapidly that I felt weak. I think about our poor faithful hearts and how many stresses they have to bear to get through this life. And for each of us, our heart is the only one we have!

Have we ever driven through our life, deciding in haste and without any forethought? I am sure the majority of us have. A few paid their impulsivity bill a long time ago, learning their lesson. Certain people are paying it still. It's like the credit in the bank. They feel that they are paying back the debt their whole life. And it seems as though all they're doing is taking care of the interest rate for the mountain is still there. Then there are some who are still making decisions without any consideration for others. They decide at a moment and then push the brakes on impulse, not looking first to see if there is somebody behind them who will get hurt because of that abrupt action. They aren't overly worried about those who are just passing through, not taking into account how a sudden danger can be tragic.

There can be people in our lives who aren't so close that they will be affected by our sudden decisions. But there may be someone closer, someone who won't have enough time to prepare and can suffer a great loss. We see impulsivity everywhere, and it seems to thrive. People in charge change plans according to the color of the sky, not taking into consideration that not all can change the rhythm of their pace in the twinkling of an eye. Sometimes, we parents tend to do that too. And if we have this characteristic, it's time to send it away with the one-way ticket to Antarctica. Be sure it will plead and assure changes just to stay. It will try to prove its presence indispensable. And for some of us, it will require tremendous energy to launch it. But it has to go away.

Sometimes, we act without thinking first and there isn't necessarily a bad outcome or something negative. But oftentimes, it's not the best way of acting. And there are people who, in their sincerity, get filled with indignation for some injustice and act impulsively. We have to understand that. Still, we should aim toward the goal of separating from impulsivity. In the long run, it does more damage than good (remember the heart).

If we do not restrain ourselves from acting before thinking, it becomes a cycle of heat-releasing energy and a catabolic destructive reaction—a pure nuclear reaction in our poor lives. We can't expect that all in our driving lane will think for us and imagine what is on our minds. When we just put our car on cruise control and then decide that we want to turn last minute, regardless of whether the reason for our decision is good or bad, we risk destroying the peace and existence of those around us.

Perhaps the driver that night had a well-founded reason to turn back. Maybe not. But it was neither the place nor the method for the action. To see someone who takes such an action going on, not conscious of the great damage he or she may have left behind is, lightly said, disturbing. I learned that word from my very dear friend. When I would be looking for an expression to describe that feeling, she would always help me, saying it.

It even seems that people who make such decisions don't care about the damage caused by their hastiness. They are accustomed to getting their way at the moment they decide. And it has to be there and then. They expect all to give obeisance to their spontaneous desires. Some have learned to keep a distance, with enough space between themselves and others, for they never know if a person will just decide to apply some abrupt maneuver. But some will be in the car of life with the person, and what can they do? Not much.

So let's take the impulsivity to the terminal, be sure to see it boarding, and then just declare *adiós para siempre*.

The Vultures

D o you remember seeing in wildlife documentaries birds who were mere observers? They would just stand there in a row and look to the right and then to the left, witnessing everything that's happening? They would be nuisances, if we didn't have something far more dangerous—the vultures.

Equipped with the latest and most accurate spying instruments available, they don't lose any time detecting a victim who is already in pain and misery. They fly on autopilot, not getting distracted by noise, pleadings, or any sight from the side. They arrive with a high-pitch sound that announces to the whole world what's happening. They bring the most valuable destructive tools—their beaks and claws—and use them, unashamed that the battle is unfair. This takes place not on the battlefield with equal opportunities but by taking advantage of the weakness and feebleness of others, when the victim is wounded or sick. No code of chivalry applies to them.

Vultures remember every detail of the victim's life, proving it with evidence that is hard to beat. Their destruction tactics are unbeatable.

The big ugly birds gorge themselves, feasting until their crops bulge, and then sit down, filled with satisfaction and half sleeping to digest their food. Their stomach's acid allows them to digest toxins from the infested carcasses that would kill other scavengers, but not them. Nothing is gross for them. Interestingly, one of the names for a group of the vultures is a committee. I do think it's a pure coincidence, but it sounds a lot like—a committee.

Now, there are vultures in every part of the world. They're found in Europe, Asia, Africa, and both Americas. Vultures from different regions have their slight differences, but the principal goal of devouring is the same.

The human heart is the same. With some slight differences, we look a lot alike. It doesn't matter where we're from. The division isn't based on the origin but on the choice to do good or to inflict pain and suffering. It's the choice between compassion and love and hardness and coldness.

We know we have vultures everywhere, but what can we do not to have them in our homes and surroundings? The authorities say they're hard to scare away. They're very persistent. But with perseverance on our side, it's possible to stay away from them. Putting pointy objects on the roofs of our homes and having a bird net helps if they've not already made their home there. If they've made their home, we should scare them away with extremely loud firework type noises.

We should protect our homes and not make them inviting for anyone who likes to devour others with words or actions. We should put up all the protections, so that such people won't feel at home there. And we must void them as much as we can and never be a part of the committee that destroys.

Just a word of reminder—vultures don't fly down like an eagle. Rather, upon landing, they announce their feast while moving around in their awkward walk and then converse over the victim deciding its fate as if its life belongs to them. The victim can sometimes go away, using the last ounce of energy and hide while trying to recover far from their presence. Whatever it takes, we must avoid being in the sight of those who devour without compassion.

Boiling Water

I was a small child when I heard this little story, but I've never forgotten it. The carrot that was hard and the egg that was soft were put together in the boiling water. The hard carrot became soft, and the raw egg became hard. The same boiling water softened one and hardened the other one. The same circumstance of life can soften some of us and harden others.

Some trials cause us to learn a new lesson. We improve upon ourselves and, seeing our mistakes, decide not to make them again. But some of us go through the same heartaches and pains again and again. Such people hurt themselves. And they hurt others. Some become so cold and hardened that it's almost impossible to move them toward anything gentle or soft. They consider it a weakness. Some even try to mock others, saying they're too weak for not being so hardened.

I am not here to point. I don't know how long the hardening process of pain and suffering in their lives was—boiling down everything noble in those people. But I know that, if we are already being boiled in some circumstance in our lives, it's better to give up the hardness and become soft and teachable.

The boiling point is considered to be at 100 degrees Celsius or 212 degrees Fahrenheit, but it can differ from that number. With increased altitude, the pressure is less, so boiling starts earlier. Under some conditions, like an uneven surface, boiling can be delayed. Some added substances can slow down the boiling point also. But eventually, it will start to boil. All of us will have to go through some boiling process too. Some will enter into it earlier, and some will have a delay. But when it comes, we will have to decide whether we want to get hardened or softened—whether we're eggs or carrots.

We children had to bring in fresh vegetables from the big gardens we had and help in the kitchen to prepare the ingredients for the very important part of the meal that precedes the main course—the soup. The main course could not be served if the soup was not there first. So the art of making good soup was essential. And the secret to a good clear broth, to which we later added other ingredients, was the long simmering time. If boiled too quickly, the process never created that typical flavor we were looking for. And if the broth was boiling for too long, it became too mushy. After a good simmering time—that is, a gentle boiling where all the flavors and aromas are blended into one—the soup was ready to be garnished with herbs or pasta, creams or sauces.

If we want to be a savor of good to those around us, we have to be simmered and to assimilate all the good things thrown at us in the pot of life. When blended together and softened to perfection, we can add some extra garnishing too. Some chose aromatic herbs, and some like it with a dash of smoked salt. Maybe none of those suit you for the list is long and very individualized. After we became a good broth, we can choose our own finishing touch.

Boiling is necessary for it destroys the bad microorganisms from the water and the food. For centuries people have known that boiling on a high temperature for enough time will disinfect water. Contaminated items were boiled in water to destroy sickness-causing microorganisms. We all are inclined to attract the germs around us. So the good cleaning with added boiling can be very beneficial for a faster recovery. Letting bad germs that became part of our lives boil down and evaporate is a very good idea.

Circumstances can be hard. We may have nobody to understand us. But we cannot become hardened. We must become people with soft or sensitive consciences—people who will grow in genuine love and care for others.

The hot boiling circumstances are all over the globe. People seem more knowledgeable, but fear and depression are actually growing more than ever. We can stand up and make a difference. I admire Mother Teresa, who dared to make a difference. She did not calculate the pros and cons but went and lived her life loving others, giving a hand and a smile. The extreme need and constant pain all around did not harden her toward human life. On the contrary, it made her even more compassionate.

All of us can do the same. We don't have to do it in the same way as her, going to India. But we can live the same way of loving, helping, reaching out, and being a blessing to all around us. Do we still remember to help our elderly neighbor with some need or we have outgrown that? Have we decided that, since we don't have time, we'll just ignore her need and pretend we did not see anything? Are we kind to the entire planet, caring about CO_2, while, at the same time, poisoning our own family with our chlorofluorocarbons and other depleting substances of anger or indifference?

I am not stoning anyone. I am the first one who cannot throw the stone. But we have to thrive and start today toward softening. We must try to regenerate our ears to hear again the low-decibel sounds we've learned to ignore in this high-pitched society.

In this boiling process, let us become the best taste-appealing people, who will have the correct texture and flavor to enhance the lives around us.

Cutting and Polishing

The gem cannot be polished without friction,
nor man perfected without trials.
—Chinese Proverb

You can be sure that I don't want the pain again and again in my life. I want to learn from every step on the road. I don't want to go repeating the process, hoping that one day in the future I will learn.

All of us have things in us that have to be chiseled away. We need this polishing, which hurts, and we certainly don't like it. And some of us go through life escaping the refining process, thinking it doesn't matter. It does! The rough edges should be taken away and polished into a smooth, shiny, and beautiful gem. Criticism, a disposition to notice and expose every defect and error, unkind judgment of others, roughness, and coarseness all should be freely given away and replaced by much nobler qualities, which will encourage a spirit of kindness, leading others to think highly and not of evil. We must speak the truth and do good to others. These aren't exactly my words, but I've heard them so many times since the childhood that I feel they are mine.

Am I there yet? Not yet, but surely I am in the process. There is such a freeing difference in the knowledge. The Bible says that the truth should set us free. I do believe that understanding and willingly accepting the changes would bring a blessing to the lives of all.

I suggest that we decide to trash all the downgrading things, purging them from our lives, and set our goals higher, aiming for the real beauty of our character. Do I propose that we should voluntarily suffer in life in order to learn? No way. I absolutely think that we should be happy and cheerful and spread joy around us. But if the circumstances become heavy and the pressure extremely high, should we let it break us or should we see how we can use that situation for our benefit?

I do love diamonds. Since my son was just a toddler, I've bought him many little samples of precious stones and gems. I was always intrigued by the process of cutting and polishing stones into shiny little objects. They are so beautiful. One of my favorites are the pink ones. They are so perfect and so strong. Yet at the same time, the pink color gives them a gentle feel—that refined perfection.

Pink diamonds are actually a product of the huge additional pressure they must pass through. They're not just any diamond, but the pink diamond—formed through pressure and then additional pressure. Did I mention the word *cutting*?

I asked a person who works with the diamonds and knows much more than I can go guessing around. He told me that with today's technology, there is a fake pink diamond on the market too. Makers of these false diamonds irradiate it and somehow produce a fake diamond.

Why would we go through a process of still painful experiences and "radiation" just to become fake people? If we're already going through some cutting experience that is grinding our soul, should we not take advantage of the process and let all that roughness and ugliness just go away? By definition, the cutting of a diamond is changing the rough stone into a faceted gem.

There are some really profound people, beautiful people. Pink diamond people around the world are those who went through the pressure and then some additional pressure and learned from it. They applied the lessons they learned to their lives and built them into the building of their personalities. They are rare. That's what makes them so precious. They don't give up in the process but, rather, come out stronger and more beautiful. They have something real to share with others. They don't have to repeat other people's stories. They have their own unique story.

Yet the results are common, with those who were already there a long time ago. And they can understand each other very well. They know the process. They can encourage each other to take the next step along the way. They can have compassion for others who are just passing through. They can give words of wisdom, sometimes. For they know that, in the pain, the words, though spoken with good intention, can be too much to bear.

Cold Formalism

The French court or the English court etiquette? The more relaxed American one? None?

I did go through an old book of etiquette many times while waiting for my daughter to finish something at school. The book was there in the office, and I didn't waste my time. I remembered so many things we had to do in the last century (that is how my children would say it) that seem out of place today. Perhaps they were a little out of place then too. There were so many codes and systems describing absolutely every movement, including how many nanograms of salt to put on the left side of the plate exactly thirty degrees above one asparagus spear. Of course, all of us know that I did superexaggerate here.

There are so many rules that some people spend years learning all of them to perfection. They do so because their calling requires it. But even the best in the field will still make some faux pas (again a French word). Every time we need some fancy word, here is the French language to help. Does that apply only when we're speaking English? I wonder whose words the French people are using when trying to impress others. No! The answer is not the first one that popped in your mind. For if you remember the history and know something of their culture, it will be very clear that they will not use words from where you thought to impress others. They are just enjoying being French.

I still remember the shock of realizing that people actually eat from polystyrene and that is the real name of the foam used to make plates and cups. Foam? Did I know all the health hazards it represented? Not at that time. Simply the thought that we were eating from foam made me classify it into a weird deed. Did I grow up in the Palace of Versailles or the Buckingham Palace? Not even close to it. But we had to follow some basic rules, and eating from foam plates was not on the menu. I did not ask if we washed them after the meal (it was before the times where we became so conscientious about protecting the environment, and the importance of not having so much waste was still in toddler's shoes). But I did wonder how those foam plates and glasses worked at weddings. In some of our cultures, plates and glasses were traditionally smashed on the floor at weddings, for good luck, I guess.

Because so many people came to visit, I started first with some elegant-looking paper plates. But with the passing of time, the obvious switch took a place—hundreds of foam plates. It was so much easier and more relaxed. There were no courses at the meals, and everyone ate with just plastic forks. It was, at first, odd and, later, normal. Whether or not the people had titles did not matter; the foam plates were on the menu. The swing went in the opposite direction.

Are manners important? Absolutely! But manners and etiquette are not the same. Etiquette can and does change according to the times and places. Things people were expected to perform at a social gathering centuries ago may seem ridiculous today. And many of those rituals were just very unnecessary. The time spent in learning them to impress others could be used in the pursuits of something of a higher goal.

Now, manners, on the other hand, are the reflection of real education. They are a reflection of kindness and perception put together and of consideration for others—a real genuine consideration. A person can never have entered a school class and be educated, and there are some with various degrees who do not have any education.

The favorite people at my table were those who did have manners but in a spontaneous way. Their manners were not calculated and artificial. Rather, they were part of who they are. The placement of forks and knives and spoons and plates can be out of harmony with the current etiquette and put on the wrong side. Maybe the charger will not be under the stack of plates, and the sophisticated golden ring will not be placed on the napkin. The elaborate centerpiece can be on the table or not. But kindness! The quick eye to help, the warmness and the absence of arrogance—these are what make the time spent together a lasting memory. We can eat white truffles from Alba and have the best etiquette possible, but if real kindness is missing, the time spent is just a vapor. It fades away quickly.

There is the other side too—those who claim they don't want to be artificial, so they just chose no manners at all. And it's like the French

Revolution—awful and dreadful. They cut off the heads of everybody who would like to be decent and mannered. We need balance. Using etiquette helps us to think about others. And it can be very pleasant if it is not the coldly followed book of rules to impress others and ourselves also. Manners are needed always—those that come from the heart. But the fact that we are putting our table (or whatever area of life) in a perfect order does not mean that we're better than those who arrange their forks as best they can on the table—on the opposite side.

That is why we've heard the counsel thousands of times that it is the heart and not the appearance that matters. So if we are using manners and show them through etiquette, it is nice and desirable for it's how it should be. But if we are hammering all around how the etiquette is more important than the person, and we judge all who do not follow every nano-step of the rules made by humankind according to the times we live in, then something is out of place. We are designed to have manners; it's not a man-made rule. It goes back for centuries. But etiquette, like fashion, is constantly changing. We cannot follow every step of these fabricated, changing ideas.

Some of us did sail in these waters. We know how fatiguing the process of following the etiquette of life can get. And there are those who are always ready to make a news report if somebody failed and put their elbows on the table or didn't direct the spoon in the right way while eating the soup. These are things that are not essential. The person can be kind, generous, and helping. But if he or she missed a detail in the process, here are the reporters. How sad to waste a whole life following the mistakes and falls of others.

Of course, I did not speak about the dining etiquette but about our lives. And though I love nice manners and I do follow etiquette when doing so is appropriate, I am very grateful for the lesson in life that helps us standing—not to focus on other people's mistakes. Rather, we should focus on our own kindness and consideration for others, which will always look nice regardless of the changing rules.

The Thorns

One day, a person approached me, asking if I had some time for she needed to ask me something. From her tone of voice and the way she looked at me, I knew it would not be a question about the trivial things but something more. Sincerely, I was tempted to postpone the conversation for I was already behind in my list of planned activities. Thankfully, I followed that little prompting from my conscience and turned back to talk to the lady.

These types of situations can be so awkward, especially during the first minute. We have to say the truth, but we don't want to say it; we don't want to hurt someone's feelings. Then the excusing stage comes; we don't want to answer the truth, for again we don't want to hurt others' feelings. It is good and necessary not to hurt other people's feelings, but holding a grudge and carrying around bitterness can be just as bad. So we have to find a loving style of clearing the way for we should not go on without doing so.

The person expressed her concern for she perceived that I wasn't as kind to her as she thought I should be. She was wondering if I had something against her. As hard as it was that first minute of going around, I am so glad for moments like this in our lives. I was clearly off the tracks, and that is not where we should be, no matter the reason. When disagreements arise, we should be quick to mend them and not wait until they rise and become the next Burj Khalifa.

The sense of a hard rock falling from the heart and a lighter walk is real. That's why we shouldn't use our energy into grudges, rather putting energy toward forgiving and loving. The outcome won't always be the expected one, but at least on our part, let's do our best.

We always had roses of many colors in our garden. I would sometimes, being a child, close my eyes in the sunshine and just smell them, trying to guess which color they were. For each rose did have a distinct scent depending on the color. And of course, they had thorns too. If you ask me to close my eyes and remember my garden from that time and particularly the roses, I will probably smile and tell you about the different colors of the flowers and their smells and how tall they were. I will probably remember the sunshine around, which doesn't mean that it never rained. But what impacted me the most, what I contemplated the longest, what was the usual is what I remember to the greatest degree. Did I enter some fantasy world of ignoring the presence of the thorns? Of course not. But the majority of people, when faced with the word *rose*, imagine the beautiful flower, not the thorns.

Thorns were there too, but it was not about them. Their presence taught us to be more cautious and careful, but we shouldn't take out the whole rosebush just because it has thorns or go in the opposite direction and ignore their presence completely.

We should enjoy the beauty of the roses, accompanied with the gratitude for their embellishing presence in our lives. We should contemplate the beautiful bees and butterflies that bring more life around the already attractive blooms. Doing so should create and elevate gratefulness and a desire to share beauty and kindness with others around us. The whole of nature gives and shares and makes our lives more pleasant. We should be in that cycle too—not just selfishly think about ourselves.

The thorns are here, and we cannot ignore them. But becoming more cautious makes as mature more and appreciate in greater measure the positive things we have around us. If we are the thorns, we should get back on track as quickly as possible and become roses. And if we got hurt by some spikes, we should learn from experience and use the lesson learned, but we shouldn't go through life in extreme fear of the sharply pointed parts of the rose. We will never experience the wholesome beauty and joy of life if we focus on the thorns.

Does the decision to focus merely on roses eliminate future hurt from the parts of life that we dread or are not willing to encounter? The perfectly clear answer is known to all of us. We know the notion of living without trials is a myth. But we can pass this path just once—dreading thorns or being grateful for the beauty of the roses that carry thorns, some more and some fewer.

I didn't read some nice stories about motivation and then put them on these pages, pretending I know it all. I do not. I was pierced sharply in this life. I was pierced with enormous thorns, if I can call them that, for they felt more like cruel harpoons launched from every direction possible and from unexpected sources. Some were so deadly that I feared for my life. Some of us know how it feels to start the day jogging, not knowing that the next phone call or written word or diagnosis can make you feel like your legs are giving up their supporting function. The days ahead are just a mourning grey all around. There is no more hope, and food seems more like a stone than a vital part of surviving. The priority is no longer whether your hair looks nice but whether you'll actually have any left. The body rejects anything that enters, as the stress is so big and the fear is so real. Those who should protect us become those we should be protected from. Even faith almost vanishes.

Thorns—none of us want them in our lives. But there comes a moment when we can decide to stand up, slowly. We can look up and see the roses again. We have a choice to stay there in our pain or become an overcomer. All of us who came through it know the feeling of gratitude, even for those wounds we would never choose by ourselves. We are not grateful to those who inflicted the wounds on us or for the cruel sickness. We are grateful for the higher ground the difficult experiences took us to for the new views and horizons opened up before us, and for the new prospects on the life we gained.

We can survive and be overcomers. We can still stand in spite of all the winds of betrayal and lies, sickness and fear, and gossiping tongues and unloving people. We can be restored and strong. Life can be full of roses of every color, each with different fragrances. We can still close our eyes on a sunny day and try to guess the color of the rose based on its smell. But this time, it's no longer a game from childhood combined with curiosity. This time, it's an entirely different experience on a more profound level. We smell the roses with an appreciation and awe we never had before. We know the difference between curiosity and gratitude. We can watch the occasional arrival of the bumblebee and the butterflies, feeling gratitude for the blue sky and the soft breeze in the trees. We can allow it all to cheer up our own spirit, being grateful to God who gives life and renews hope when we think that all is gone.

Stubbornness

This story is old—a couple of centuries old—but I am pretty sure it's very relevant for some of us today. There was a man who had a wife who always wanted her word to be the last and to be obeyed. The poor husband had to submit to her word and requirements and follow her instructions. He had to let her be right about everything.

One day, while sitting in front of the house, the couple looked up and saw a beautiful formation of cranes flying over the house. Up ahead of the formation, a big beautiful crane led the route.

The wife exclaimed, "See that crane that flies first? He is mine."

"No, wife. He is the elder, and he leads others. I am the elder, so he is mine."

"He's not yours but mine," answered the wife. And here the argument started to heat up. Finally, the wife declared, "He is mine, and if not, I will die."

"Then die," said the husband. "For once, let my word be heard too."

The woman lay down and, for the whole night, pretended to be dead.

In the morning, the husband said, "Wake up, or will I call the women" (who in that time prepared bodies for funerals) "so they can prepare you."

She opened her eyes and asked, "Is he mine?"

"No, he is not," answered the husband.

"Then let them prepare me."

So they came.

The husband, pretending he was mourning, came to her ear and whispered, "Stand up, or they will now go to announce your death."

"Is the first bird mine?" she asked, whispering.

"No, he is not yours," the answer came.

"Then let them announce me."

95

"Stand up for the priest will come, and the people will take you to the burial ground."

"Is the bird mine?"

"No."

"Then let them take me."

The people took her to the graveyard, and while the last prayer was said, the man knelt down beside his wife and muttered in her ear, "Stand up. Don't you see that they will bury you?"

"Is the bird mine then?" she asked again.

"It is not," the husband replied.

"Then let me be taken to the ground," she said.

The priest took a handful of dirt and threw it on the coffin.

The husband, seeing that this will not stop, said to the priest and to the people, "Go home. I will come. Now just let me stay with her a little bit more."

Then he told her through the coffin, "Woman, what are you doing? Come out and stop with this!"

The answer came in the form of a question. "Is the bird mine then?"

"It is not."

"Then take them all home and let them drink and eat for my soul for I will die."

The husband was outraged. He pulled up the casket lid and said, "It is enough."

"Is the bird mine then?" asked the wife.

"It is yours. Just stop this nonsense," replied the husband.

The words that come to our mind after this story may be *bizarre, odd, exaggerated, unreal,* or *strange.* But let's be honest with ourselves. If we think about our own experiences looking back, weren't they just as trivial in the beginning? Wasn't it because of somebody's stubbornness that disagreements become a real tragedy? It can be our obstinacy or someone else's that caused lifelong scars that should not be there.

Like always, we have to separate the healthy dose of inflexibility and determination that is needed to survive from the ill stubbornness that destroys other people around us. To win "just because" and the "my-way-or-the-highway" style of thinking are not the goal.

We need stubbornness and a high dose of inflexibility when we are pushed to do something wrong that we know we should not do. We also need a high dose of determination and perseverance so that nothing will stop us from achieving our good and noble goals.

But what about the lifestyles where the people involved can be happy or bearable only if their points of view are followed? They make life miserable for everyone around in order to feel their own supremacy. We cannot love by force. But some think that, if they force you enough or scare you, then finally all will be just fine. That kind of love and life is cheap. Love is awakened by love and not by force. Respect is earned not pulled out by fear.

How happy was that wife to know that the bird was hers if that bird was miles and miles away already? Do we just need to get our way and then we will be good for someone? It is mere selfishness in its most bizarre form.

Sadly, there are people around us who get their way and walk triumphantly around in their plumage, showing that the tough hand can bring good results in the end. And maybe it is so. My question is, What was the price? Who had to yield his or her own personality and wishes, his or her own dreams and individuality to fit somebody's ego?

Michel de Montaigne was one of the most significant philosophers of the French Renaissance. In his *Essais*, published in 1580, he states the following: "It is a disaster that wisdom forbids you to be satisfied with yourself and always sends you away dissatisfied and fearful, whereas stubbornness and foolhardiness fill their hosts with joy and assurance."

If we were or are stubborn in a negative way, let's make a place for personal growth and soothing away that foolhardiness. It will take some time, but we are here to win and, every day, to learn new trails, climbing the mountain of personal growth. If we have to submit ourselves to a giant stubbornness around us, it's time to let those who are stubborn see that they can have their own way by themselves. Do they want to have a bird that is flying over their head? They can have it. And enjoy it. By themselves. We do not have to be pulled inside their world of selfish obstinacy.

Darkness

A pasha gave orders to carry lamps in the night. The following evening, a man was found without the light. Upon being asked where was his lamp, he pointed toward it proudly. The angry officer told him that he needed to put a candle in it. A lamp without a candle is useless. The next night the officer found the same man walking in darkness. How could he disobey the orders? The officer yelled this question. But the man just showed the lamp and the candle. He had done all that he was told to do. The officer shouted again, explaining that the candle needed to be burning in order to give light.

"Nobody told me that," answered the man.

I had to walk home from school, like everybody else at that time. We would go to school in the mornings for one month, followed by a month of going to school in the afternoon. It is a horrible way of doing things for people who love routine, but here I am. I survived it. Those short winter days that quickly became dark were not my favorite. My parents always tried to come to meet me at least half of the way. Still, I remember having all kinds of scary ideas while walking as rapidly as I could.

My mom tried to explain to me that everything was the same as it was during the day; only the light was missing. Now that was the key to all—the absence of light.

Maybe everything was the same—the same houses and streets, the same dogs behind the same fences. But it was not the same. At least it wasn't for me. Everything was bigger. The negative things were bigger. Taller shadows caused major fears. The same trees whose shade we loved to play under in the summer looked so scary with their long shadows. And when I saw my house lightened all around, I got new energy and just ran to my safe place—to the light and love.

Can the presence or absence of light make such a difference in our lives?

Shakespeare, in *The Merchant of Venice*, wrote, "How far that little candle throws his beams! So shines a good deed in a weary world."

We can see darkness all around us. And if we focus on it, it will pull us into it. Everything looks bigger and scarier in the dark. Things that we could handle during the daylight become mysterious, heavy, tall, and frightening.

Some of us can easily come out from the darkness once we realize that there is another option—that there is a light ahead and a better place. But some, who were in the darkness for a long time, need to get accustomed to the light little by little. They need to take it step by step, accompanied by understanding and patience.

There are those who love to stay in the darkness, and we have to respect that, but we do not have to stay there with them. We have to be that candle that will shine the light around and, at the same time, make our lives richer. If they hate, we cannot. We cannot be just lamps without candle or candles without light. Our lives cannot be a simple display in the lamp. The fire has to start. And it must give light. We have to love. If others damage, we cannot. We have to restore. We cannot use the same way of thinking as being in the darkness, for there, everything seems so unreal.

And what about our own dusty, dark corners of life that we neglected and somehow do not want to think about them? Clean those corners up and light a good light in them too. Let every aspect of ourselves become well lit and a safe place for us and for those who are around us. Some will need a fast deep cleaning, but some will need more delicate handling. Then let the light shines for our own sake and not for others. When they see our own lives bright and in absence of darkness, they will want to try it also. That's the way to shine the light. We can't be trying to save others from their own lives while we are in our own darkness. Now is the moment to light up that hope and never again let it be turned off. And what if it gets dimmed and turned down? Then take the matches and light it up again.

The Dry Prose

There is nothing wrong with prose. It is essential. But some of us need a little contrast. We need some poetry. Certain lives are simply encircled in the same charts of to-do lists. We should add some lines of poetry to their list, so they can read the poetry and cheer up for a second before returning to their straightforward way of living without too much decoration.

I am very grateful to my friends who did that with me when it was most needed. I do love poetry, but I am very selective. And I don't like too much decoration in everyday talk. But in this poetry talking now, I am using it as a metaphor for brightening someone's life with glittering things that are maybe not the most essential things for survival but a little extra luxury—maybe even a laughable nothingness that still adds to a person's well-being.

A friend would take us out just so we could laugh about completely nonessential things, in order to relax and recharge the batteries for the next not-so-decorated step. That is adding some poetry to the lives of others or others to ours. Our loved ones, who we sometimes consider dry prose, when not with us, we realize, may be Nobel Prize-worthy poetry.

I'm talking about friends who send us gifts just to surprise us or send us a letter in the mailbox, knowing that it is still very special for us though we talk daily on the phone. This is poetry, in spite of the prose, and it refills our hearts. We could not go on without it.

We can learn to see more poetry in life around us. It is there in the birds who come to our window in the morning or in the flowers that are there also. Many small things make up our days, and days make years, which are our lives. So we should see every step, every minute like a very essential gift and learn to enjoy it more.

Adding music to a poem gives us a song. We have to see things through glasses of gratitude and love. I'm talking about real giving love, not the kind of moody sentimentalism that society has come to call love.

We can't expect great things to be accomplished if we aren't appreciating all the small things. This is especially true for those of us who have gone through some very trying times. We can see the nothingness of life, of properties, of titles—we know that they can be gone as if they never existed in just a masher of seconds. And here the veil comes off our eyes, and every moment becomes a gift worth celebrating. The good and the bad—all can be used for our good. Not everyone can understand this for hearing about it is not the same as walking through it and survive. Our story cannot be a copy of someone's life or narration. It has to be our own testimony. We can and must use the same words that have already been used for centuries. And maybe we can add some wise sayings of people who have already gone through life's tribulations. But the main thread of the story has to be unique.

We do not have to buy a bouquet of flowers to be happy and, until then, just grumble. We can admire the flowers in the fields and add that intonation in our hearts of gratitude and poetry. We can take flowers that we wanted for ourselves to someone else, and seeing their happiness will add double poetry. It's nice to have the poetry just for us and our circle where we feel comfortable, but we should reach out a little farther, where is not so comfortable. We should try to put some smiles on weary faces and gives songs to those who've heard nothing but prose for so many years it has become their way of living.

I have many dear friends who share their time and means and give medical help to the people in need. They take a couple of days in a year and go to some remote and not-so-remote places to perform surgeries, to give free medication, free glasses, and free dental care. They bring poetry to the people who cannot pay them back, and that adds the music of the symphonic orchestra—for there is no selfishness behind it. These things and services are given without expecting anything in return. Now they do get their pay too—the people's gratefulness. Some of us aren't going so far, but we can reach as many here around us. Without trumpeting our services, we can spontaneously help others along the road to have some extra glitter sometimes. The glitters and the poetry are not the same as the regular prose help and support they need. They are just stanzas or two of some salt sprinkling on their unseasoned life.

Emily Dickinson wrote a poem that says:

> If I can stop one heart from breaking,
> I shall not live in vain;
> If I can ease one life from aching,
> Or cool one pain,
> Or help one fainting robin
> Unto his nest again,
> I shall not live in vain.

What a simple, true message for all of us. Let's try to bring some poetry and maybe even some chords of music just to embellish someone's life for a moment.

A Domino Effect

A domino effect or chain reaction is the cumulative effect produced when one event sets off a chain of similar events. The term is best known as a mechanical effect and is used as an analogy to a falling row of dominoes. That is how the online dictionary defines it.

Domino games originated in China, and I can imagine these old Chinese men calmly using their strategy and tactics while playing dominoes. Now for the domino effect, I remember my parents sitting with me and building the chain on the table. Then the honor and privilege of starting the chain reaction were given to me. I just loved those days of my childhood. Of course, it was very interesting to me. So we built the chain again and again.

How different can be the emotion upon seeing the same effect years later in other circumstances. I am not talking about chain reactions that can start with one thing going wrong and then unexpectedly another, and before we know it, from every side wrong things just keep happening. The case I want to mention involves a chain reaction that is well planned and measured to the yoctogram (which is just one septillionth of a gram). That's a very impressive measuring. Only one scale can do it. And those who start this type of chain reaction belong to the very specific species of chameleons. That special brand of lizards possesses extra speed; they eject their tongues with a highly adjustable ability, able to cover large areas with one flick.

And while scientists are still discovering their answers to every important detail and classification of the mentioned sort, I am just going to share what I saw—or, better said, what I didn't even have time to see. It happened so fast. Have you ever seen how slowly chameleons roll out their tongues? Of course not. Not in real life. Perhaps you've seen this on a slow-motion video. But in reality, it happens so fast. Every time. One can almost consider Einstein's theory that nothing can travel faster than the speed of light (in a vacuum) not to be true—when you consider those tongues. Chameleons can pretend to just be sitting around minding their own field of interest (that could be their work perhaps). Then, with the speed of a flash, they extend their long tongues and grab their victim. And it happens so quickly that nobody really pays attention to it—except for the poor victim.

Chameleons plan every detail and organize their attack just like a domino chain. Then, with the speed of a light unperceived and unseen, they gently Touch the first domino. And the poor victim's dominos just fall one after another.

That gentle touch is very difficult to analyze or describe. That starting soft touch of planned chain reaction can begin with a benign question of supposed consideration for others but put in a very clever way. Chameleons should study physics (if they could) because their formulation and timing of reactions is on the perfect level of quarks and leptons.

They can swallow their victims without even blinking. They remain just as calm as they were before they pushed the first domino or extended their tongues, continuing to look in all directions with those supereyes. Their eyes focus independently. They have the ability to talk to a person but, at the same time, observe their surroundings, looking for the next victim. The unique gift of observing two different objects simultaneously belongs to them. This skill can be used as a blessing—especially for us mothers, it seems like a needed skill. But in the case of the chameleons, it is not motivated with the same virtuous desire. And in spite of the small size of the creature, it can see very far. Even things that should not be on their list of consideration are being observed—in detail.

When we say *chameleon*, we usually think about their ability to change colors and patterns. Not all of them do it. But in general, that is how we like to imagine them. It is their most distinctive characteristic. Some can change colors from yellow, orange, green, blue, red, and even some light tones of turquoise, reminding us of the beautiful gemstone that was esteemed for centuries as a holy stone. These camouflaged starters of chain reactions can be red or yellow, just like the context of their environments, and they can even be considered holy.

I am very glad that, back in Europe, we didn't have any crocodiles or any of their closest family members. I remember the first time I saw these lizards—having landed in a country full of them. They were on the trees, outside and inside the houses, on the trails, and even on the beaches. One would think that, here, we could just rest beside the long, white-sanded beaches with the beautiful turquoise water. But this brand of two focused eyes was right there, hanging from the palm trees. The lizards would be in the windows too—just so you didn't feel unobserved. And I was assured they were just so cute while hanging from the ceilings inside some homes. I instantly identified them as crocodiles. They were smaller maybe, but still crocodiles—at least for me. I was really scared of them. I screamed and ran every time I saw them. That was going against every picture of normality created in my head for years before that. After years of disgust and distress upon seeing them, I guess my poor defense system just gave in. Finally, I started to ignore them.

The day came—actually, it was a night—when I walked into the kitchen and saw that crocodile thing on my ceiling. I could not scream. I had a baby. How did that thing get inside? There was a screen on every window, and the doors were closed. That lizard found its way of entering even the privacy of my own house. Now I know that it was not a chameleon, but they belong to the same family. And by my own taxonomy, I added them to the bigger lizard family of crocodiles. Finally the day came when, due to circumstances, there was no one to take out the lizard. I took the broom and removed this creature. And then I returned, passing under the triumphal arch. From that day on, I would not scream anymore. Instead, I would take out the broom if the lizard were in my house or on my window. And if I saw it outside, I would just ignore it, no longer letting it ruin my peace.

Sadly, there are many around us who will gladly launch the domino effect in the lives of people around them constantly. They do this a very subtle way, grabbing whoever they want with their tongues. We cannot scream every time we see them. It's immature and tiring. If we don't want these people in our lives, we should put a screen and close the doors. That way, we'll know we did our part in not being close to their superseeing eyes and sticky tongues. And if they push the first domino in our lives, and everything moves downward, we have to stand up and remake our lives, ignoring the chameleons though they change their color to turquoise.

Human Philosophy

Human opinions and philosophy are almost the same, but we could start a philosophy class about that. I loved my philosophy class. Or better said, I did not love it, so I discussed my dislike with the professor of philosophy, and that made me love it. (Now this is a philosophical thought.) And during those times, we didn't choose answers from a, b, or c options. Rather, we stood up and used our brains. I am not criticizing the multiple-choice, cookie-cutter finished, and polished answer. I'm just having some nostalgia for the times where we used the good old oratory system.

And the poor professor. We called him a philosopher, and that was just a plain name for someone who did nothing but live in the clouds of his own invented ideas. Or on the next level, it's someone who lives on borrowed ideas and questions about life—as if there were not enough questions already. He tried to solve these riddles as the earth rotated and the days passed away.

He looked very unhappy. He tried to follow all of the so-called big philosophers, and he just seemed to be pulled in many directions. I am sorry for him and do not wish to degrade him or anyone else. I do have many dear friends with degrees in philosophy, and I know that there is a sincere wish to find the answers. But we can read all of the great philosophers trying to follow them, but many of them led very unbalanced lives. They were tormented to find answers they could not uncover, and some ended very tragically. They were the same flesh and bones that came to its end like every other human. We should ask questions that are really important and simplify the answers in accordance with our daily need.

Some postmodern philosophers say that there is nothing else to be discovered, nothing else to be debated. Humans just proved they are not bigger than their Creator. They're not even equal.

I'm not wishing to offend but to prompt people to think about some of the questions philosophy asks. There are grandmothers who had more common sense than that. And the field of philosophy is highly recognized as wisdom that there's no chance of using common sense against it. It seems to me that it's useless, like trying to discover wheels when they were discovered more than 5,500 years ago. The answers are known, but the human mind many times refuses the simple answer. My mathematics professor always said, "Why simplify if it can be complicated?" Some questions are just not to be found, but we have to live our best and give our best.

Multitudes today are swaying from one end of human ideas to the other extreme. In my opinion, the saddest of all is that many people do not cultivate or have their own criteria and opinions. They are just loudly repeating what is popular—not to mention that they like to add heavy philosophical words that not even they understand just to impress the crowd. They are easily influenced by anyone and anything. They don't have their own yardstick but are always borrowing one from someone else. They hear some motivational speech, and they become the captain of the ship. But after a few days, they see another ship passing by and, immediately, without having to think or look carefully, they abandon the ship until the next one catches their eye. That's how they live.

All of us have realized at some point in our lives that we're on board the wrong vessel. But we've had to grow and learn to discern and be wise, asking ourselves, By which human opinions do I want to travel? Just because a philosophy is popular or loud doesn't mean it's right for us or for anyone else. Look back at history, and you'll see that the popular was not the best always.

We have a privilege to use our reasoning abilities and develop our own tastes that can and should be unique. The insecurity of not knowing whether or not we fit in here or there will go away. It will give us enough strength and grace to say no to the things we don't consider edifying or merely aren't suitable for us—because we will feel comfortable in our own skin. We do not spend every moment copying someone but, rather, we focus on developing our own qualities.

Some men who were wise left us a tremendous legacy of their ideas that are good to know. I did and still love to learn from them. But we cannot live other people's lives. We cannot go wasting our time trying to fit into the fragile human philosophy. We don't want to be someone else. There is a purpose for each of us. Let's stand to fulfill our own.

The Fall

Are we perfect? Have we never failed and never fallen? It would be very nice if that were true for my belief is, why go forty years through the desert if we can make it in just two weeks? But for the sake of mercy, we are permitted to learn from our mistakes, stand up, and go on.

Now, this theme is the favorite one for those who love to fall. Some like to claim, who are we to judge, and then they devise how to fall and claim that we all fall and need mercy. Right, but I strongly believe that we have to put our bar high—in every aspect of life. So our aims should be toward that goal. Like the little child who learns to walk and falls less and less often while he or she is maturing and having more and more experience, we should do the same. It's not that we should plan to fall. Rather, if it happens, we should quickly stand up and go on, still aiming toward the goal.

Life on the cycle of constant, planned falling can be exhausting and devastating—usually for those who are around.

We've all heard hundreds of times about Edison's perseverance, but if you look around carefully, you will find many examples of perseverance—especially in nature. Victor Hugo was convinced that perseverance was the secret of all triumphs.

I don't want to go naming the classical examples of people who failed in every aspect of life—being refused, rejected, called stupid and good-for-nothing, and told they'd never achieve anything—only to become famous leaders, inventors, professors, businesspeople, and so on.

So we do have proof that falling does not have to define our lives. There are falls on another level too. Morally, our characters can fall. There are not many examples of that kind of perseverance and victory on the internet today. But there are some. In every culture and all around the globe, there are survivors of the fall. Some fell heavily. Some fell not so obviously, and they learned to quickly jump up, clean the dust and dirt off, and decide to get to the goal.

Some could not jump back so easily because of the hurt suffered. But they did put all their effort into a comeback, and they persevered toward the finish line.

Some did not have a good start. There was nobody to guide them and teach them with love and perseverance. They had to learn on their own. Others had a good start but stumbled somewhere in the middle of the runway, distracted by something on the side. We don't know what could be hidden there deep underneath. But the message is clear—don't fall and stay down. Stand up and put your eyes toward the prize. The finish line has to be passed, and the victory celebrated.

There once was a speedy hare who bragged about how fast he could run. Tired of hearing him boast, Slow and Steady the tortoise, challenged him to a race. All the animals in the forest gathered to watch.

Hare ran down the road for a while and then and paused to rest. He looked back at Slow and Steady and cried out, "How do you expect to win this race when you are walking along at your slow, slow pace?"

Hare stretched himself out alongside the road and fell asleep, thinking, *There is plenty of time to relax.*

Slow and Steady walked and walked. He never stopped until he came to the finish line. The animals who were watching cheered so loudly for the tortoise that they woke up Hare. Hare stretched and yawned and began to run again, but it was too late. The tortoise was over the line.

After that, Hare always reminded himself, *Don't brag about your lightning pace, for Slow and Steady won the race!*

In this classic Aesop's fable, there is no fall, but perseverance is the message. Don't look at the impossibility of the circumstances. Instead, mark your goal high and do not stop until you pass the finish line.

I was still back in Europe when I was learning to pass my driver's test. I knew I would pass the test because I was driving well and had learned everything in the book. Now, we didn't have permit driver's licenses like they do here, and our books were thick. Some students, in order to pass the exam, had to change the tire. Others had to drive at night. Some had to drive to a place they'd never driven before, which could be another city. And of course, the perfect parking in which you turned the wheel just three times was required. I don't remember in that time having wheels that turned easily like the steering wheels of today. But I was almost sure I would pass.

And I did not. The system was not set up so you could miss thirty out of a hundred and you were still good to drive. It was either you passed or you didn't.

I was in denial. My father came to the testing site, and we sat in his car. He told me it was nothing—that I had to go inside and submit a petition for the next exam. Everything inside in me was saying that I didn't want it now. Maybe I would do it again later. But he firmly repeated that the sooner I did it the better. I went just for the reason of pure obedience, not that of hope. This time I went with less confidence in myself, but I did pass all the exams. I was so glad that I didn't postpone it.

Sometimes we need a push from a kind soul who cares. Sometimes, we can push ourselves. At others times, we need the combination of the two. The thought of feeling comfortable in our own pain down there and not willing to move can be the force that we have to fight against. No. There is no time to waste down there in the dust of our own misfortune and fall. There's not time to plan how to, if, and when we stand up. We have to stand up immediately—feeling it or not—for this time we will make it.

Bad Outcomes

There is a story about a man who was so unlucky that nobody could help him.

One day, a rich man decided to see for himself if that was true. He took a bag full of golden coins and put it on the bridge where the unlucky man had to pass.

When the poor man came close to the bridge, he murmured, "So many times I have crossed this bridge. Let me see this time if I can walk on it without looking." So he crossed the bridge with his eyes closed.

Many of us go through life accompanied by some discouraging situations and burdens. To some, this may appear to be a constant reality. At the same time, it seems that, for others, the red carpet is rolled out under their feet. And here is where we give up. Tired and exhausted, we lose sight of the goals we once had. The stars no longer seem to shine for us, promising dreams. Rather, they seem to have become distant flickering lights in the cold darkness around us. Maybe we should just give in and give up.

There is no reason to live just to survive. We compromise the principles we once held high and just live from day to day, focusing on the trivial. It almost hurts to think or to hold the rope of hope. The tears flow no more, and the dry face, once full of life, becomes the indicator of broken dreams. Bitterness can take place, and it's worse than anything for it eats up its host to the bones.

The truth is that nobody can fully understand another person's hardship or suffering. We can try. We can be compassionate and loving, but the burden of agonizing pain is unique for every person. There is no one way to cure these ailments that works for all.

We can lift our heads and learn from the survivors—from those who were defeated again and again. We can learn from those who fell but stood

111

up, those who were broken in pieces but chose to be made anew, those who refused to just survive from day to day deciding instead to live an abundant life that brings hope. Hope brings to life faith, without which we cannot function. It brings about living faith.

What about when all is gone with the wind and every plan has failed? I'm sure many of us failed the plan A and the B too. Some of us settled with the plan D. But what if there is no more hope, for it seems that we have failed even the plan Z? The good news is that there are other languages to learn—languages that have more letters waiting just for us. Of course, I am not talking about learning Hungarian or Arabic or even Japanese (though it's a good idea to learn any other language). Rather, I'm referring to a new perspective, a new language of talking to ourselves and others—a language of hope. Using this new perspective, we can stand up and use the broken pieces of our plans to make a beautiful new mosaic that will exceed all our expectations and make us alive again.

We can toss away bitterness and replace it with the joy. Do we cry in the meantime? Yes, it shows that we have a heart—a heart that is made of flesh and not from steel. Man and woman, there is nothing bad in crying. The tears can wash our eyes and make us see clearly.

And let's not forget one day, when we recognize those tears in others, to remember the intensity of the pain we felt when we were at that place.

Like the song says, we can be in May or in the September of our lives, maybe even November or December. But keep up what the old Latin speakers were saying—nil desperandum (never despair).

Did we despair? Many times. But no more. And if the old habit comes back, let's show it the back door of our heart. And let's be sure to lock it well afterward. Maybe we should acquire a new heavy-duty lock to replace the old one that did not serve its purpose well.

Marcus Tullius Cicero is considered to be one of the greatest Roman orators and prose stylists of his time. He accomplished great things by the standards of the world, but he wisely concluded, "Omnium rerum principia parva sunt" (The beginnings of all things are small). And that saying should be combined with the German folk saying, "Besser spät als nie" (Better late than never).

Some can start just small. Perhaps don't even stand up but crawl. And that is a beginning. Anything is better than staying where we are, defeated and in desperation. Some can walk only a step a day, but it is a beginning. And it has to be encouraged. Then, as the days go by and we become stronger, we can run. Run toward the goal. Run toward that high aim that we somehow lost in the detours of life.

A long time ago, there was a king who was defeated in battle. Discouraged, he lay in the hay in a hiding place. He noticed a spider on the wall. Not having anything else to look for, he observed the small creature. The spider was crawling to a place, trying to bring a thread to the other side but could not make it and fell back. The spider fell once. Then the spider crawled back up a second time. He fell again. But he kept coming back. Upward the spider went—ten times. The king was counting, intrigued by this interesting display of perseverance in spite of a bad outcome. Finally, the eleventh time, the spider was rewarded for his not giving up. He put the thread where it had to go. And the king, encouraged by this life lesson, decided to stand up and fight until the victory was won.

Greed and Selfishness

Midas, in Greek mythology the king of Phrygia, was known for his foolishness and greed. According to the myth, Midas found the wandering Silenus. For his kind treatment of Silenus, Midas was rewarded by Dionysus with a wish. The king wished that all he touched might turn to gold, but when his food became gold and he nearly starved to death as a result, he realized his error.

Do all of us have a need for more? Probably so. Our clothes wear out. Our children grow out of theirs. Modern technology can help, but it's still man-made so gets to its end too. Appliances are, it seems to me, made to last for just one day after the warranty expires. Our homes always need some extra repair too.

Believe it or not, there are serious movements around this planet suggesting some rather odd ways to save the world. And some of them are sure that we should not use water to wash our clothing but freeze it in the freezer to kill the germs and to prolong the lives of our wardrobes. We are free beings, and our thoughts should never be legislated. So I can surely not share my sympathies with the idea but still would never prohibit others from their own concepts of happiness. I am one of those who believes that water washes away the dirt. And I will not discuss ways to save the planet but say that, in spite all the attempts, we still have some real needs. So needing some new things is not covetousness but a necessity.

Where is the line between the real need and avarice? Does having nice things and some extras means we're greedy? I don't think so. Greed is when the desire for having more and more obsesses us and makes us forget about those who are around us. It's when we play unfairly and low just to get what we want. The worst ones still pretend to play by the rules. No one's wish will be granted if that deprives him or her of having more.

In Proverbs, the Bible says clearly that, though a person invites you to eat with him, if he is stingy, you should not crave his delicacies, for he is a hypocrite. Such a person they will count every morsel he or she gives you and will regret it.

People who are stingy go through life saving and saving even more, not enjoying a moment. I grew up seeing older folks who were very careful in their spending, saving and working hard. They came through two world wars and lived through situations that we never did and hopefully never will. So they lived with precaution, saving all they could. Those people created for us an easier life, and I will never call them stingy.

But in all times and in all places, we have that type of greediness that will hurt others—the type that always wants to get more. The courtrooms are full every day because of battles over who will have to give less and who will retain more. And since the court brings a decision, those involved feel they fulfilled their obligations. Adios to the conscience that goes above and beyond the paperwork and should do right in spite of our crooked views. Contracts are being signed under hundreds and hundreds of small illegible words. People have to sign for they are in need. But the huge companies take advantage of this necessity and pay the smallest amount required. And if not for the law, they would pay people even less. I am almost sure that some would even return to the slave system if that were possible. Banks are not happy just to get some percentage; the bigger the need and the deeper the pit, the higher the interest they charge. Is it just my own pondering or would all the debate over child labor overseas decrease if some people would be less—let's call it like it is—greedy? I personally know individuals and families who give more and have successful companies here around their own communities. They are a blessing to the society around them, and at the same time, they are being blessed.

We do live in an insatiable society that teaches us that it is very well and necessary to be greedy too—of course not in that same terminology. We hear words that are more embellished and more appealing to our own selfish nature. A human being is the same through the ages. The curtain goes up and down, and the scenery is changed a little. But the drama is the same. The same character traits are still relevant today. We can change their names and add some scientific research, but in the end, it is the battle between good and evil, between lower and higher, and between noble and ignoble.

You surely remember the story about the man who killed his hen who laid a golden egg every day. He assumed she had more inside her, and he couldn't wait to get all that gold. Sadly, he did not understand that he had just enough for every day. Now he had nothing left. He realized it too late.

A long time ago, we were told, "All day long he" (the covetous) "is craving, while the righteous gives and does not hold back."

Many years ago in the Ottoman Empire, a rich man lost his bag of money. So he sent for a messenger to go around the city. In every street it was announced that whoever found the bag would get a hundred coins of gold.

An older peasant found the bag and quickly took it to the man who'd lost it. The other suddenly became so sad for he did not want to part from his hundred coins of gold that he'd promised as a reward. So he tried to find a way to keep it. He smiled and said, "I see that you already took out the reward so I do not have to. For there were eight hundred coins, and now I see just seven hundred. Thank you so much."

The poor peasant felt so ill, trying to prove that he had never taken anything out of the bag.

But the other insisted that he had. So finally they went to see the judge.

Fortunately, the judge was wise and saw immediately what the real matter was. So he said, "I see that both of you are right. The problem is that we have the wrong bag. The bag found is not your bag for this one has seven hundred coins inside, and the one you lost had eight hundred. Peasant, take home that bag for this is not his bag. But wait until the real owner comes. For the real owner lost only seven hundred gold coins."

Forgetfulness

Ivo Andrić (Иво Андрић) was a novelist, poet and short story writer who won the Nobel Prize in literature in 1961. He said that nothing connects us so closely as the trials and hardships lived and survived together. We can identify more easily with others who came from the same affliction and hurt as we did. But there is a tendency in the human heart to forget sometimes more than it should.

The peasant was taking his horse and ass to the farmer's market. Both had a load to carry. The donkey got very fatigued, so he asked the horse to help him to alleviate his load just a little for the horse was bigger and stronger. Both were carrying the same amount of the burden, even though the horse was bigger in size.

The horse responded harshly, "I have enough of my own." And he would not talk about it anymore.

Sighing, the donkey tried to bear the burden, but it was just too much for him. The poor animal was beaten to stand up, but in vain, for he exhaled his last breath.

The owner took the load from the ass and put it on the horse, with the addition of the donkey's fur that the man did not want to waste.

The horse was repenting by now. "With a little help," he murmured to himself, "I could alleviated his burden and saved him from death. Now I have to carry all the load and his fur too."

To some degree, we all have to go through life with a load. Some get a lighter load and some get a life-crushing burden. Those with the lighter burdens are prone to ignore those who walk sighing beside them under the burden. They can see their fellows being drained of life's energy due to the extra load put on them. Or they can hear their sighing and pleas for help to alleviate the burden. But they don't want to consider giving any kind of help. They have their own things to do and think of, so they walk away, forgetting. They consider their role much more essential than that of their lowly fellow human beings, who lack significance.

The wolf grabbed the sheep and with wolfish gluttony, he swallowed it. But the bone stuck in his throat. That generated a lot of pain and misery, despair and fear. He asked every animal to help him, but they all refused and wished for him to die.

Here came the crane, the long-necked bird, who was known for her skills and meekness. The wolf also asked her to help him. He promised a good and generous reward for all the effort she would put into saving his life. She immediately helped him.

When the wolf was freed from all the danger and went on to live his life, the crane waited for the reward and requested it.

"I am surprised that you are expecting recompense! Aren't you satisfied that you saved your head from the wolf's strong jaws? Go away and do not come close to me anymore if your life is dear to you!" cried the wolf loudly.

This is another group of people who forget. They come to the point of having a bone that is stuck in their life and is suffocating them with desperation, anguish, hopelessness, pain, distress, and unhappiness. They lose hope and give up, lose heart and get discouraged. And a kind heart is touched by their misery and reaches out to them with friendliness and kindness—so cordial and warm, accessible and approachable. That is, until the bone is taken out. Then those who previously were plagued by the bone are almost proud about it having been stuck there.

Some of us have seen this more frequently than the others, but all of us have seen a person on a sickbed. Even the most wolf-natured people become somehow lamblike, and we almost anticipate that maybe this sickness did change their hearts. Maybe they will no longer eat the lambs anymore. But isn't this human nature so *intéressant*?

We do not have to go trumpeting around our past or the bones once stuck in our throats. But there deep inside, some transformation should happen as a result of the trials we've been through—and that transformation should be be manifested on the outside. The story could finish in a different manner.

The wolf could make use of the lessons life gives to all of us through hard times. He could think not just about how to get out of the situation but about how to come out of it better—even if that meant leaving behind his whole nature and starting a transformation. He could honor the word *given* and be touched by the kindness of the crane and possibly want to be kind like her too. He would do it in his own way, but he would no longer be known for the negative but for the good he became. And that would make such a huge impact on the whole community of animals. Maybe the other animals would be touched by this huge transformation and, first, give it time just to be sure. But then they would follow the same path of wanting to improve, making their own lives and the lives of those around them better.

The lessons in life are sometimes harder and sometimes easier. But if we neglect the lessons there are to gain from the experiences on our path and just go on, we will get to the finish line in a miserable state. We cannot forget the lessons learned. We have to keep them fresh (the lessons not the experiences) in our characters and build on them with the next ones.

While we are in a trial, we see others around us and think, How can people be so indifferent? But when our situation is improved, do we forget too? Are we indifferent also? Do we mind our own load, ignoring the suffering along the path? Did we forget how nice it was to know that somebody cared? When it's not our own skin (or throat) on the line, then somehow we measure the pain with a different scale. And sometimes life will allow us to go unpunished and never feel the fear anymore, like the wolf. The people who helped us will be forgotten, and no lessons will have been learned. It's our choice. Mediocrity is one of those choices.

We should find a balance, giving more weight to what is more valuable to us. Do we live our lives and use people when we need them and forget them when we don't? Do we pretend to be changed when it's necessary and forget the lessons we should apply? Or should we have more altruistic aspirations and views on life?

Let's finish as we started with nice words of hope. If we do not forget and we learn our lesson, having gratitude in our hearts, we will expand our relationships with people who have done the same—like the little mouse and the lion. You've probably heard the story many times before. There are probably some variations in every language. But the lesson is the same.

While the lion was sleeping, the little mouse ran over him. The lion woke up and wanted to eat him. The mouse begged the lion to have mercy on him. "Please have mercy on me, and I will one day pay you back."

The lion started laughing for it was so impossible and funny to consider a mouse saving a lion that he decided to release the captive.

After a while, the lion was in trouble. He fell in a net that hunters had left for the animals. The little mouse heard the despairing roars of the lion.

He came as quickly as he could. (He didn't go to sleep first and then go think about whether he could find some free space on his timetable while the other was crying for help.) The little fellow worked hard chewing on the net until the lion was free.

And the mouse said, "You were laughing, not believing that the weak could help the strong too."

Isn't this a much better outcome for all of us? And the wise Aesop (Αἴσωπος) wrote the three little fables for even then, centuries ago, there existed the people who forgot and the ones who did not.

Death

Can that be possible? To stand in death? Yes, if you have lived standing. When somebody died in our village, that was sad. I think it was like in Bible times, where there were ladies who went to every funeral and were there just to weep. Only hearing their loud expressions of grief made us all cry. I never wanted to go to funerals. Our mom was the delegation representing our family. I did not understand the value of standing even in death, until last year, when my grandmother, after almost reaching a hundred, died. She died peacefully, like she lived, with dignity and standing. She was born the year when the Austro-Hungarian Empire fell apart. So her parents became citizens of the new country, whose language they did not even speak. She survived the Second World War and became a widow. My grandfather, being a German, fought on the German side. My other grandfather was on the side of the Allies. War is never, ever good. It separates, destroys, and damages.

The new country was made again. There were new laws and regulations. There wasn't justice. They took away all the properties from the Germans and gave them to the refugees. My mother still keeps some old, yellowish, falling apart papers showing that my grandfather was being pardoned so he was permitted to stay in his old house. He paid rent to the refugees who got his house. And his love was the horses—the huge beautiful horses that, of course, had to be given away too. My grandmother told me stories of people who came and had never seen electricity, so they made jokes about the chandeliers in the house. They took the wooden floors apart so they could make a fire for they had never seen a stove. She was always repeating that some of them who took the houses from our uncles and aunts still had the same curtains in the home—decades later. I do not wish to speak badly against the refugees, for it had to be terrible to lose everything and everyone. Yet it was unjust for the others too. If humankind would simply follow the law of neighborly love and care, how many tears would never flow?

They did not have a lot of communication in the time of the war, so I do not know how this exactly happened, and surely I will not go to investigate it. My mother knows the whole story, though. The war was raging. Many of the families were ripped apart. Some of our family members were dying of hunger in Russian concentration camps. Years passed. I think my grandfather's first wife just thought she couldn't live alone, not knowing what was happening and maybe imagining the worst. She remarried. Great was the surprise for him hearing about this after the war. So he married my grandmother. They had to start from the ground up. Hard work was what they had to put into their lives. Finally, crushed down by the great injustice he bore, he became very sick and died.

But my grandmother kept on. I remember her house. It was very important for our ladies to maintain the gardens beautifully. There were flowers in the front yard and vegetable gardens in the backyard. The big fields outside the towns belonged to the men to work them. How the house looked said a lot about a woman. It told whether she was neat and a good housekeeper or whether she was lazy and not so clean—whether she was a good wife and a mother. A good cook was, in my opinion, a universal quality. Some were better than the others. But all knew how to cook. They used basic ingredients that were cultivated in the garden—no recipes and measuring cups.

My grandma was almost dismayed if she saw weeds in the garden. The way to maintain a garden was not a huge buzzing work carried out every once in a while to show off and take pictures. Actually, it was a silent work, done year after year every morning. She weeded every day, not waiting for weeding to become a huge project, impossible to manage, but doing it while the weeds were easy to pull out.

This is something like our lives. The flower beds of our lives should be maintained every day; we should pull out the weeds when they are just small and easier to get to. We should regularly add new flowers, watering and nourishing them daily, so we can be a beautiful, fragrant garden for the people around us. Can that job be finished once and for all? As long as we breathe, there will grow ugly weeds in our lives. But cultivating the habit of pulling them out immediately will make us a place of beauty and encouragement for others.

Every spring, my grandmother painted all the windows and the house. And she would do everything very carefully and with perfection. She always said that how we make things around us shows a lot about our character. It defines us. At the usual time, she would come into the house to prepare lunch. Sleeping habits? No weekends or lazy days. Early to bed and early to rise. Things had to be put back in their places after being used for we had to be able to find them, if necessary, "in the black of the night."

Being older, she had a lady who helped her to cook and clean, but she still wanted to be useful. I have in my freezer the last bag of walnuts she cleaned, from one of the trees in my parents' house. Older people (and by the way, all of us are heading in that direction) do not want to be put on the table like a vase. Nor do they want to be put on constant care, where we don't let them even think for themselves. They need to be and feel useful. Sadly, our skin gets more raisin-like and our movements become slower. But are we lesser people just because of that? Does our need to be loved, respected, and needed disappear? If we do not have the same tastes as the new generation, should we be eliminated? Should we be cast to the side, justifying our deeds with the huge medicine intake we provide for them?

I remember, in Germany, there was a lady who paid me (like a summer job) just to sit down for two hours and listen to her stories. The amount she paid me for those two hours I still cannot be paid here even for a whole day of work. Human beings are desperate to be heard and loved. The woman who paid me to listen had a son who was very well educated in the schools and had a perfect profession. He put his parents in a very expensive apartment, where they could just push a button and be downstairs in the supermarket made just for the elderly people who lived there. Or if they needed to buy more medication, the pharmacy was just an elevator ride away. It was a perfectly organized system, where nobody had to talk to anyone—a dream for every sophisticated mind.

And then comes death. Everything is calculated. Nobody has a right to come in and hold your hand in the last minutes of your life—because... I will not go to those waters. But reading the Bible I saw this pattern of old patriarchs dying and calling their families. Surrounded by loved ones, they said goodbye and asked forgiveness or blessing. This was the way they departed.

My grandmother called all who had to come and told them her last words. She encouraged them. Somebody called to say that my grandmother had died, so my mother went home on the first airplane she could get.

But my grandmother hadn't died. She was waiting for my mom. She was waiting so they could embrace each other. Slowly her speech became weaker, and she went to sleep. She died in her sleep. I remembered that she'd told me many times she would die peacefully in her sleep. And she did.

For the first time ever in my life, I dared to think about death that is more like a standing than a death. There are no words to comfort the loss. I do believe that we are not created to die but to live. And all that death around us is just a reminder of how fragile the human is. We cannot make or create life on our own. We need more than just a vain human philosophy. We need a guiding hand to guide us through the rough seas of life and brings us safely to the harbor.

The Muddy Ponds

There are some beautiful artificial ponds that are maintained regularly very well. And some people like them. But it requires an extra investment of time and means. I am not talking here about our artificial, nicely maintained ponds but of the lowlands, breathing with humidity, mud, and mosquitos.

Without speculating how some of us ended up there, let's just start with the fact that here we are and that it's time to leave this muddy pond behind.

Some still don't realize how bad the high humidity that evaporates from the mud is for us—how damaging it is to our health and to the health of our loved ones as well. The problem with high humidity making us feel hotter is not just that we are more uncomfortable. Our core temperature is actually rising, and our bodies compensate by working harder and harder to cool us down.

Dehydration depletes the body of water needed for sweating and thickens the blood, requiring more pressure to pump it through the body, thus forcing the heart to make an unusually great effort. As blood goes to the external surface of the body, less goes to the muscles, the brain, and other organs. We become weaker physically, and fatigue occurs more quickly. Mental faculties may also be negatively affected. We become less alert.

High humidity causes dust mite populations to grow faster and mold colonies also. So here we have respiratory problems and allergy sufferings. And then, instead of addressing the cause, we just take some products to alleviate the symptoms and signs. All the while, the source is still there—right in front of us. And it will not go away. In the summertime, the muddy, humid swamp becomes even more dangerous, with its mosquitos.

I've heard twice in my life that we should not kill, so the mosquitos should be protected. Whoever invented that theory should really investigate mosquitos. They do not just suck our blood that our body has to work hard to make. They are primary vectors for major human diseases, such as yellow fever, malaria, and dengue fever, which together infect hundreds of millions of humans worldwide and kill millions each year.

Mosquitoes spread disease agents. They do not cause diseases directly. When feeding, a mosquito pierces the skin like a needle and injects saliva into our skin. This allows the disease-causing agent to enter our bodies. So they are not just feeding on someone's hard work and life; they are leaving a legacy of germs that cause sickness.

Some can have serious symptoms of respiratory distress that will not improve by itself. Being surrounded by mosquitos is an everyday risk too.

So we have to identify the lowlands of our lives. Maybe it's the people who pull us down? Maybe it's our surroundings, infested with the heaviness of mosquitos that are draining our blood? And here we have to see what we can do about that. Some will maybe invest in heavy equipment, draining away the source of the allergies. Some will need to leave behind those surroundings. And some will maybe bring large loads of good soil and try to lift up the place. In all cases, it is hard work. But it will still lead to improvement.

The house of our lives should be built with the best material and surrounded by the best environment. Let's be surrounded by positive, encouraging people—friends who don't drain us, leaving us with the toxins and sickness of negativism. And let's also work on being the one who will be the refreshment and not the sickness for our friends and neighbors.

In extreme cases of inability to remove the muddy atmosphere or to move away from the bad, we can always learn from the lotus. With its roots based in mud, the lotus submerges itself every night into murky river water, and undeterred by its dirty environment, it miraculously reblooms the next morning without residue on its petals. The lotus flower blooms most beautifully from the deepest, darkest, and thickest mud. The lotus is a symbol of purity of the body, speech, and mind in some religions. With such refusal to accept defeat, it's almost impossible not to associate this flower with unwavering faith and gigantic hope. If the lotus can, we can make it also.

Ungratefulness

We've all helped someone (hopefully) along the road of life or were helped in some time of need. The difference is in the way we help.

Growing up, I never heard about stores where people can take things they don't want anymore and then others come and don't just take these items but, rather, pay for them. I still have some personal doubts about the concept. It can be good; but it also can be not so good.

We become tempted to get accustomed to seeing people in need and just ignoring them, thinking what is not good for us anymore should be perfect for them. And sadly, they come to believe the same.

One thing is to have something that you could still use but, for various reasons, don't want it anymore and then decide to give to someone who would really need it. All of us who have children know they can outgrow clothing that was barely put on. So we have items they wore once or twice for a special occasion, maybe a little more, which are still in good condition. We cannot keep these items anymore, for we need space. But we don't want to throw them away, so we give them to someone who really can use them. That is perfectly normal, and I'm not talking about that. But if the condition of the article is miserable, then we should put ourselves on the other side of the fence and be honest. Would we like to receive that if we were in the same need?

I read about the lady who had a real need for a new dress. It was in the time when people had to go to a seamstress to get a new outfit. Since the clothing wasn't abundant like it is today, the fabric had to be high quality and more expensive than today's fabric. It had to last longer. So when she needed a new dress, it was not to remain à la mode but to replace the item that was worn out. Then she heard about someone in real need and decided to give her newly acquired fabric to the person, while she would use her old dress a little longer. She explained that giving someone something of value, something new, makes him or her feel better and more valuable too. It was enough for the poor person in need to feel miserable for not having basic things. Why show her that she belongs "down there"? The golden rule is still valid: Do to others as you would like them do to you.

Or what about some of us who like to display with a flourishing ceremony when we are helping someone or giving for some good cause? What happens after the grand drapes are closed and the applause is stilled? Perhaps we love the stage and the loud approval of the clapping. That's all well and good. But do we remain compassionate and quick to help when there is no one to give us applause? Do we give with the right hand and with the left ring the bells? Do we have a feeling of superiority? Do we expect a person to be forever an ever grateful on every step of the path and to repeat his or her gratitude and follow us like a benefactor?

An old saying from the Balkans says, "Gladnog ne teši, već nahrani" (Do not console the hungry but give him something to eat). Some of us are ready to teach others life lessons and tell them how sorry we are for them, but our outreach remains only words—pure cold theory.

Can we give not expecting anything back? Are we moved by love or selfishness when we reach out to others? As Albert Camus said, "C'est cela l'amour, tout donner, tout sacrifier sans espoir de retour" (That is love, to give away everything, to sacrifice everything, without expecting anything in return). Now that wasn't his original idea. It had stood for centuries already.

And then we get to the other side. We do all of this, but some people think they deserve to have our best because we have more than they do. Whatever we have, they are here in line to wait for the splitting of the goods. They don't even consider saying thank you, for greed and jealousy are motivating them. If somebody gives them their best, they find a reason to complain, saying that it is easy for the giver for they have much. If the person is genuinely kind, they try to decode the supposed meaning behind it. If ignored, they will still find a way to release their poison of doubt. Such people are impossible to please—or to help.

An old German saying refers to "aus einer Mücke einen Elefanten Machen" (an elephant made out of a mosquito). And that goes for both sides—for all of us.

My grandparents lost their home and properties for the government at that time thought that they had more than enough so it had to be given to those who did not have anything. It cost them health and, in the end, life too. I'm not advocating some kind of socialism where all belongs to everyone and those who do not work will reap the benefits of those who do. I'm talking about good old sharing and helping those we see in our midst who need our help but still want to retain dignity—in spite of their needs or circumstances.

Here we can encounter some people who are kind and seemingly caring. But when the object of their mission becomes independent and not needy of their help, some become resentful—to varying degrees. This comes to ugliness too sometimes.

Then there are those who, if not helped anymore, become bitter and criticizing. All the good that was given to them becomes insignificant compared to their disappointment.

And the truth is it can be unfair for both sides. Maybe sincerity was involved, but something just went wrong. Then should we be ungrateful? Never. The sun that shined on us this whole life shined on the mean ones too. We should see it as a benefit for us. We have to be grateful for every small or great blessing along the way. If it was just for a day, then we are grateful for the provision on that day. If it is for the whole year, then we should be thankful for that.

Our goal is not to change the world but to become better today than we were yesterday and better tomorrow than we are today. If we were ungrateful, let us become more aware of responding kindly. And if we were giving selfishly, let's become more delicate and compassionate toward others who do have enough hardships.

Human Opinions

A man and his son were once going with their donkey to a market. As they were walking, a countryman passed them and said, "You fools, what is a donkey for but to ride upon?"

So the man put the boy on the donkey, and they went on their way. But soon they passed a group of men, one of whom said, "See that lazy youngster. He lets his father walk while he rides."

So the man ordered his boy to get off and got on himself. But they hadn't gone far when they passed two women, one of whom said to the other, "Shame on that lazy lout to let his poor little son trudge along."

Well, the man didn't know what to do. At last, he took his boy up before him on the donkey. By this time, they had come to the town, and the passersby began to jeer and point at them. The man stopped and asked what they were scoffing at.

The men said, "Aren't you ashamed of yourself for overloading that poor donkey of yours and your hulking son?"

The man and boy got off and tried to think about what to do. They thought and they thought, till at last they cut down a pole, tied the donkey's feet to it, and raised the pole and the donkey to their shoulders. They went along amid the laughter of all who met them, till they came to the market bridge—when the donkey, getting one of his feet loose, kicked out and caused the boy to drop his end of the pole. In the struggle, the donkey fell over the bridge, and his forefeet being tied together, he was drowned.

"That will teach you," said an old man who had followed them. "Please all, and you will please none."

All of us have heard some variation of this story. We go through our lives pleasing and pretending—like "The Great Pretender." Now let's be clear. I do think that children should be taught to please their parents and obey, instead of dreading them and doing what they say *just because*. The happiness of sharing with others our accomplishments where we are pleased with the outcome and making others happy is not bad at all. Today we tend toward this Freudian opinion that, if you do something nice for others, it has to do with some hidden selfishness, expecting a plan. I totally disagree. I had a nice childhood, and encouraging each other and pleasing our parents is not sick. The self-oriented society and its never-ending theories analyzing every arrival of the impulse on the neurotransmitter and how it affects our daily life is exhausting.

I am talking here about pleasing people in an unhealthy way. All of us, the majority at least, have tried and failed on that one. Then we see the other end of the spectrum, where people won't do anything kind, for they do not care. I am just calling for a normal, commonsense balance.

Here I was—a modern mom. I think, *Forget about that old-fashioned way*. I ordered every magazine and book about raising children. Books being my super love, it was so easy for me to swallow them, digest and incorporate their advice in my daily life. And looking back, I really think I deserve some prize for putting completely opposite opinions (hundreds of them) together to work. It was quite an accomplishment. Now I would do it so differently. At least I know why they do not work.

Each one of us is a completely different individual. We each have our own needs and pace. We need to form our homes and families in the beauty of our own unique taste. Good for the people who wrote the books about how to. But being just a mortal, I do not dare say to others this is how to. I can write to encourage the positive, the kind, and the good. I can share some stories. But I cannot make the map of life for anyone. It is not my job—expert or layman.

How many broken homes are there, for suddenly our expectations are measured by the postmodern society, where there is no relevant truth but still somehow we follow every opposite opinion of the experts. If my spouse does not do like the book says, then I will whine and give him or her the silent treatment. If we do not live like characters in the movies live, then it is time for "Arrivederci Roma." What if we would just use our short years, which actually fly away so quickly, giving love and trying to make the best for others around us, not whining and expecting that we are here to be served the way the books are telling us? What if the time in the home should be just a relaxing welcome, where we try to give and not expect anything—where all can feel at ease because *there is no place like home*?

Wrong Ways of Teaching

I loved biochemistry. Actually, I loved history, Latin, and art (though I never advanced too much in the area of the painting. I am probably a good candidate for the National Medal of Arts for the baby stage of a drawing). Later, I loved surgery and psychiatry. Why? Because the professors who taught me the classes were so inspiring.

I would wake up at 3:00 or 4:00 a.m. to get ready for class. I read additional material beyond the required material, not to show off but because my curiosity was eager to know more about the subject. It looked so interesting and so broad and just easy. It was very important to me to be extra neat in my notes on those classes and to listen to every word. The professors knew how to wake up the curiosity (of which I've always had and still have enough) to learn on our own. They challenged us to go higher than the answers around us. I am privileged to have met many bright minds and know them on my journey. Remembering them sometimes makes me nostalgic, when I compare it to the shallowness I see many times around. And that same shallowness sometimes, sadly, represents intelligence and education.

The biochemistry professor had a doctoral degree in pharmacy and was very organized. She would write everything down on the board and classify things in different columns, with different colors and would draw a concept of everything so we could understand it. Though she had a doctoral degree (like all our professors), if she saw we hadn't quite mastered the prerequisite material, she would go back to the basics—back to the elementary level and work it with us, using examples from everyday life that were familiar to us. When she was sure we understood, she would build up the subject she had to teach. How can somebody not like biochemistry? I thought.

There were some examples of pure academics too—no curiosity, no motivation. They were just learning the volumes of the assigned tasks.

132

They came to the amphitheater, took their seats, heard the exposition, and didn't even remembering their names the next school year. They were very educated and had in-depth knowledge, but didn't have that extra kindling that lit the fire of curiosity and learning type of teaching.

Sadly I did pick up some bad examples too that perhaps works for that time but should not be used to teach. I used these methods in my life, thinking it was the correct way. Since it gave results for me, it must be the effective way, I reasoned wrongly. My first piano teacher would have a pen in her hand and would hit our fingers with all her might if we played wrong. Somehow, I do like piano playing, and deep down, I am grateful for that teaching too. But some got discouraged and just quit.

We are all made of dust and have equal value. But at the same time, we are fearfully and wonderfully made. We are very unique in our personalities. Good teaching requires a lot of tact and wisdom. I'm not talking here about teaching in schools and institutions. Rather, I'm referring to dealing with people around us. We have to wake up people's curiosity and interest in the subject, not merely give orders. We have to be careful with the more sensitive people in our lives and not break their lives with our correctness. We should be careful not to crush their uniqueness and right to think differently. We do not have the right to be other people's conscience or radar control.

If we have to share some information that's for their good, let it always be said in a loving and kind way. I am sure that we can find a way of conveying the message that will suit their needs in the best possible way.

The Seriousness

A cheerful heart is the best medicine. No scientific studies are needed to research this statement for people have known it to be true for centuries. But since researchers already have conducted many studies, we can just put it in a little bit more schooled way. Laughter strengthens our immune system, boosts our mood, diminishes our pain, and protects us from the damaging effects of stress. Actually, that is a very chewed-down and simplified conclusion of all the research into laughter.

There is a time for everything under the heaven, but I am sure that we need some more healthy laughter. We grew up eating meals in courses. We did not talk all at the same time, but the conversation was flowing. Maybe there was some silence, but we were still comfortable.

But I will always remember the occasion where we were invited to visit another home for dinner. The soup was served. Not a word. The main course came, and then the salad, followed by the dessert. Not a word. Perfect seriousness. I was just counting the seconds to go home. And there I sat, daydreaming about inviting people to my home but making them welcome and cozy.

Fortunately, there were fewer courses than at my aunt's place, who had an endless list of the food we all loved. But my memories of her place are the best. There, we talked or listened and laughed. We laughed a lot. And the food was good too—homemade and just perfect. We felt at home and relaxed. At the same time, our deportment reflected that required at the table.

I lived in a country where you just had to move the lips on the right or left side (the choice was totally yours) but not more than a nanometer. If somebody was determined to notice it, he or she could as well as carry a high-resolution microscope with him or her. And that was defined as a smile—a polite smile, the highest achievement of human civilization. It was an ultrarefined greeting method. If you did more, than that you could look suspicious. And of course, that was not the goal of your travel in the suburban train. Now that, compared to my early childhood, where we had to greet people politely on the street, created a big confusion.

But even there with all that seriousness, when knowing people better, behind the walls of their homes, human nature (which is very much the same everywhere) would just come up. The so serious, no-feelings-involved individuals were just as vulnerable as the loudest nations in this world. They knew how to laugh and how to cry. They wanted to be loved and to love. They were hurt and resentful. They complained and had compassion. They shared their stories and hopes.

They became dear friends. They were beautiful people. And they knew that they are missing something in their lives and that what was missing was not a private jet or the newest Ferrari. They had all that. They had all the seriousness and organization of this world but needed some cheerfulness. Maybe a lack of purpose, too, was present, but this was the ice-breaking moment they needed—just to laugh and to interact on a normal human basis. And I do repeat, I'm referring to healthy laughter. Definitively, behind every good thing, there comes its counterfeit too. I'm talking about simple laughter that comes from pure thoughts.

Laughter decreases stress hormones, and we are for sure bombarded with the stress and stress-related conditions all the time. Laughter improves the flow of the blood to our hearts, which decreases potential heart attacks. It increases pain, releases tension, and strengthens relationships. Why would we not laugh more often?

There are people who are a little bit on the shy side. Give them more time and just be kind to them. We aren't the same, and I do respect seriousness too. Since there is a time for everything, there is a time for solemnity. I am the first to practice it also. But this is an invitation to put a little more on the joyful side of the scales of balance. We do not have to make the world laugh, but we can at least laugh with the people around us—our families and friends.

I remember as a child entering some places where just the mere look of the building made me feel scared and silent. I didn't always have the same approach toward people that I haven't now. But I did conclude that everyone needed a smile. Some are so deeply seared that no smile will move them, but they are the minority. The majority is just hiding behind the mask of seriousness. It makes their life seem easier. They make no compromises and have no attachments of any kind—not even to their neighbors.

Charles Dickens said that there is nothing in the world so irresistibly contagious as laughter and good humor. So the next time you want to display just a nanometer of politeness, put a smile on the serious face and try to spread some joy and positive laughter around you. Remember at the same time that there is a time and place for everything. So do it if the occasion is appropriate. And if it's not, then just give a polite smile that is a little more than the usual one—one that comes from your heart. Maybe you need to decrease your stress hormones or just to release tension. Perhaps somebody around is not expecting a smile from you, so you can just surprise him or her.

The Changes Around Us

Not long ago, I saw some pictures from a place I used to go to school as a small child. I just could not believe what I saw. They were painting some religious themes, and there was a whole slide displaying the pride of the achievement. Every picture revolved around church life and school blended together. The parents seemed so delighted with their children's progress in church life.

Let me explain why awe was my reaction. When I was at that same school years ago, I had been mocked for believing in God—buy everyone, from the teachers to the students. But because I was a good student, some teachers turned away from the insults, and they became my favorite ones. I still remember my first teacher. She had the most perfect handwriting a human can have. And she could draw like only few can.

Then there were the students. One was leading the group. She would give the others ideas about what to do with me after classes. For example, she would suggest they find some big earthworms and put them in my hair. Or they would, under her direction, take umbrellas and poke me with them while I was running home. She was the granddaughter of a person who had received my grandfather's house after the Second World War. Since the government took away everything from the Germans, who had to give their homes and property to the refugees who did not have anything, they were the new owners of everything. They got new positions in government offices too. Is there a better way to get people to follow and be loyal? In addition, government apartments were later secured for their children.

In spite of all that treatment, I was always chosen by the class to be in the leadership position. Fortunately, I did not attend that school with the person who was so mean and her friends for long. All her acquaintances came from the same line. Their grandparents had received the beautiful properties that had previously belonged to Germans, until the end of the Second World War.

The older people nominally belonged to some churches, but their membership seemed more on the superstition side than on the faith side. And the postwar generation was completely educated that no God was the absolute truth. Those who believed in God were considered second-class or, better said, fifth-grade citizens. Actually, three figures were the pillars of that kind of society—Marx; Darwin; and, believe it or not, Freud.

Some years ago I would give my opinion about that subject, but I do not classify it important anymore. There are so many higher aims to focus on.

I was the only one in the whole school who had some different beliefs. I never talked about them or promoted them. But it did somehow bother the others.

When there is a system imposed and everybody pretends to be delighted with it, the individuals who don't just bow down are considered bones in the throat. They can be honest and the most polite and hardest working people on the planet. Yet they are obstacles to the "paradise" the leadership desires—where nobody questions and everybody nods and no one ever lacks exaggerated praise and flattery. With some added news of the lowest kind of triple-face pretenders, it is the utopia of those kinds of societies.

But as time passed, people knew me or my parents better, and we did build some very nice friendships. The old system was slowly coming to its end. New changes were taking place, but I was no longer there to witness it. So in my mind, the old rigid structure was the only depiction of that place that I still had.

Seeing the changes that had happened in the same place where I had been mocked for believing in God's existence, as if my belief were just absurd, was strange. I never promoted my beliefs. If I was asked, I answered but I never pushed my belief system on others. Some of my friends did have questions, and we discussed my beliefs, but that took place outside the classroom. Now, the pendulum had way overflown to the opposite side. The school has become overly religious—again I'm not referring to the personal but to the collective level—just like it had once been overly anti-religion on a corporate level.

I did reconnect with my first teacher a couple of years ago for I heard that she moved away and was very sick. We spoke a couple of times, and I sent her some packages just to encourage her and show my gratefulness for what she'd taught me. She cried and asked me for forgiveness. She did not have to ask me for that, for I loved her and I had forgiven her a long time ago, understanding that she was under a lot of pressure. Her husband was the director of the school for many years, and they were just followed the rules from the top. They simply followed the changes around them. She was sobbing on the phone, telling me that her parents always had a Christmas tree and that she had grown up in that atmosphere. She blamed herself for not standing up to defend me. I never told her whether or not I observed Christmas. Nor had I said whether I believe that doing so was the same as believing in God. But she wanted to show that she was sorry. She said I was the only one who called her after she was moved to a nursing home. For me, it was very sad when she died for no phone or technology can replace the human touch or embrace of love. All the gifts of this world are just a note compared to a composition of the personal presence. But at the same time, how wonderful is the feeling when forgiveness and love take a place in our hearts long before that parting moment.

I always think that, in life, when bad has to happen and we have to choose sides, we should always chose the side of the good. It's better to be oppressed than to oppress. It's better to be robbed than to rob. It's better to be falsely accused than to accuse falsely. It's better to be wronged than to wrong others. I still opt for not having to go through any of this, but we all know that, in this life, we do have to go through at least some gravel walking—without shoes. Even if seemingly an eternity is passing and no results are seen, it is still better to stay on the right side.

When others realize that they have done us wrong and try to see how to make it right, we won't worry about that, for we won't have lived our lives in regret and confusion or in bitterness and anger. Maybe we did for a short time, but it won't have marked our lives permanently.

I remember my grandmother and others who had to adjust to huge changes in a short time but stayed on their paths. They came to their finish lines having accomplished the most in life. They arrived without regret. When the pendulum swings when least expected and brings with it huge changes, are we going to stand our ground or swing with it? The best way is to stay on the path, moving toward our goal and adjusting to the circumstances, while sacrificing as little as possible of our personal objectives.

Lack of Wisdom

I was a very good student at school, but at the same time, I detested it. I couldn't wait to come home. Home was, for me, freedom. And if you think I mean freedom to do whatever I wanted, no, that wasn't the case. We were at liberty to do whatever we wanted but within certain boundaries.

At school, I almost always knew the answer, but I never rushed to raise my hand to answer. I left that to others. But if questioned, I would give an answer. I loved the teachers who usually were not the favorite ones because they demanded more. I could not stand the teachers who were not so intelligent but pretended to be. One of them was teaching German, and her pronunciation was just so bad. It was grammatically correct but not phonetically. Worst of all, the teacher who we'd had before was such a beautiful person—very kind and elegant. She spoke perfect German. So I somehow compared this teacher to the previous one and could not pretend that she was my favorite. I never could with anyone. To worsen the situation, she was quite rough and rude.

Being immature, I pronounced my German correctly but putting emphasis on the sounds she could not articulate well, and that created an obvious cold war between us. She had to give me good grades, but she liked to add some extra heavy material just for me. Actually it turned out good for I needed it later in the life. We can learn from everything in life. If nothing else, learn from such situations that this is not how we want to be when we grow up.

In that time, the only way to eat was around the table with the family. Here we discussed what had happened during the day, and I shared all my new findings. Or I just did not want to share, for I thought it was nothing special. We could talk openly about our opinions. Even though the whole world accepted something one way or teachers said it another way, for my parents it was very important to let us express our own opinions. They always taught us respect and obedience but gave us free will too. And looking back, I couldn't be more grateful for that.

I am realizing that it was not school but my home that put every foundation in place for me. It was home that instilled my love for learning and for books. I was curious about everything and encouraged by my parents to find answers. Every day at noon, my grandmother would listen to a radio program that had a classical music quiz—for ages. I still remember it started with Brahms's *Hungarian Dance No. 5*. Like it or not, I grew up with it, which later helped me with my music education. Traveling, discovering and discussing—all that together helped greatly to open the horizons for me. We had many visitors in our home, and we kids were always part of our parents' conversations with them. Likes sponges, we listened and learned.

Not everything was flowing so rosy and optimistic always. We went through hardships and fear, through loss and war. But that too was a building block of who we are. That added some new aspects of our perspective on life. When you see human suffering and dying around you, if there is any humanity left in you, you appreciate life on a different scale.

I loved history, and I could memorize, it seemed to me, every important date from the entire history book. But I couldn't memorize the poems. I just could not learn them. Then my mother had to learn them with me. She would help me and naturally learn it in the process. When the big day was almost here, I would be sure I wouldn't know the poem I have been working on the next day. I saw a long time ago Victor Borge talking about learning Japanese and putting the cassette under the pillow, hoping thusly to accomplish the goal. That was a comedy and intended for people to laugh, but for me, that is how I hoped to learn my poem—by putting the book under the pillow. Somehow I always did well, but it was a pure miracle. Not until high school did I start to appreciate poetry. A friend loaned me her book by Rabindranath Tagore. I just loved his poems. I have not mentioned him or thought about his books until just recently.

So that was a good combination of the knowledge I got in the school and my home. I could probably survive without knowing about "Inferno" in Dante Alighieri's *Divine Comedy* or the role of Mozart in the creating and making popular the piano concerto. Maybe I could even live well without knowing what year man allegedly stepped on the moon or what marked the end of the Hellenistic period. Like it or not, yes, we can live without algebra too. But there is something we cannot live well without, and it has some qualities that are familiar with knowledge. But all the knowledge of this world cannot fill its place.

Maybe we live in a post-Newtonian conception of physics. And since Antoine-Laurent de Lavoisier, chemistry has branched into organic chemistry, inorganic chemistry, analytical chemistry, physical chemistry, and biochemistry. It sounds so educated and sophisticated, but all that is nothing without wisdom.

And wisdom does not come from books. We all had to learn the same things in school, but many did not take advantage of that opportunity. Some just could not learn, and that's fine. Not everybody can understand Latin or French. Some of us were born in homes where multiple languages were spoken, so we just had to learn in order to survive. And adding one more thing to the list, for some of us, learning was easy, but not so for others. Others related better to some other areas that maybe we did not understand so well. But to live without gaining wisdom is a lost path.

In the Holocaust's systematic murder, the biggest part was having the most brilliant minds. The so-called scientific medical investigations on poor victims were not conducted by savage tribes centuries ago led by Genghis Khan. The perpetrators were the very cream of the scientific world. I remember my biology professor saying that most scientific facts in the field of medicine we know came from that research—or what we should call that wickedness. Groups of people were tested to determine how long people could go without sleep, without food, without air—ugly things that I do not want to write about. And lucent minds were there, just taking notes. With their hands, they wrote the human suffering they witnessed on their notepads. After that, they had to go and listen to Richard Wagner (mostly). They were listening to classical music after a workday—intended just for the "higher minds."

Is mere knowledge enough? Aristotle said that educating the mind without educating the heart is no education at all. Our goal should be intelligence and character together as the real education. If we have to choose, I would rather take character over the pure facts of intelligence.

A while ago, I was listening to a superfluous exposition about ethics. I was almost sure that the person speaking didn't even know the real origin of the word *ethics* but probably had some degree on the subject without having the basis in real life. Since the word is so widely used today, we all are trying to impress others with our knowledge of it—not making the connection in our brain that ethics is not a mere list of rules to comply with in order to relate to others but our characters. Doesn't the Greek word for ethics actually mean relating to one's character? If I talk ethics to others, I better myself live by it. And that involves every shelf in the inventory of our lives.

Beware of the mediocrity becoming empowered and the experts.

The picture that captivated people's hearts was their already beloved president sitting at the desk with his son playing under it. You know who I'm talking about. It was not the only time this happened, but it was the only time a picture was taken. That room and desk was a government property and a very valuable piece of it for it was the Resolute Desk. A gift from Queen Victoria years ago, the desk was built from pieces of the rescued Arctic discovery vessel. It had been used by almost every president in the Oval Office. Now talking about strict rules of persevering, that piece of furniture could never seem to do so enough for something like that has to be carefully taken care of. And they did, but they mixed the rules with the heart and common sense. Did that president have an excellent education and knowledge? Did he have the responsibility of leaving a good example? Yes, and he had power and authority too. Yet he did not become a favorite by trumpeting his impressive degrees but by showing his more human side. He identified more with people on their level, and though he represented the country, he did not lose his heart.

Thinking about our short lives, I wonder how can we ever think big about ourselves? We are just so clearly nothing as fragile human beings. We need a bigger wisdom to guide us for on our own, we are just like blades of grass that come and go. Our lives are precious gifts. We must live them wisely. We may think that, because we know how to argue or how to impress people with our laurels, we are on the side of wisdom. Maybe we even have our notepads (like the scientists in the concentration camps), showing our smartness and power, but this is not true wisdom. "Science is organized knowledge, wisdom is organized life," said Immanuel Kant.

I realized that the old sayings or proverbs in every language are more or less the same. That is because we are more or less the same. They bear a lot of the simple folk wisdom all cultures have. They are a product of human life and nature observed. And surprisingly, they are short and simple.

I do not believe that they can be copyrighted, for nobody can copyright wisdom. There are just so many words in our human language to describe the same characteristics. The Proverbs from the Bible are the best. Everything else said about wisdom is simple a repetition of what is said there in some form or another.

We can be on different marks on our journey. Some may have started recently, some may be way advanced, and some may be in the between. But like Confucius said, "It does not matter how slowly you go as long as you do not stop."

Envy and Jealousy

Mankind are tolerant of the praises of others as long as each hearer thinks that he can do as well or nearly as well himself, but, when the speaker rises above him, jealousy is aroused and he begins to be incredulous.
—Thucydides

Thucydides wrote the *History of the Peloponnesian War.* He was a historian and an Athenian general during the war. I am convinced that he spoke from experience talking about envy. Almost certainly many were envying his place, wanting it for themselves.

We are talking here about that feeling of unhappiness and resentfulness induced by someone else's qualities, possessions, or some desirable attribute belonging to them. These feelings of envy and jealousy are very close to each other. The emotion of coveting what someone else has mixed with the feeling related to fear that something you have will be taken away by someone else.

We can be surprised by sudden changes of so-called friends, not just in adversity but in prosperity too. We hear it like a refrain that real friends are known in times of trouble. But what about the moment when something positive unexpectedly happens to an old friend? Is there real genuine rejoicing or are the lips moving in one way pronouncing gladness and delight while the heart begins to cherish some strange feelings? Why him or her and not me? All of us can have these kinds of temptations, but should we let them develop to their full size or just pluck them out immediately, the moment they start germinating? Very few have the elevated characteristic of being joyful with the ones who are rejoicing and crying with the ones who are sad.

It's almost as if people feel they are sitting on thrones. As long as a "nobody" appears who won't interfere with their mediocrity, they're fine.

But if somebody appears who has more knowledge than they do or is loved by others or has whatever characteristic they desire, they actually would like the torment to start. It's the Wars of the Roses.

They can dwell on the subject for hours and more. It pulls them inside that vortex of self-pity and envy. Some pretty ugly things happened in history because of envy—over and over again. Humankind somehow does not want to learn, and the majority likes mediocrity. Sometimes it can be detected on people's faces and in their behavior, but sometimes people are able to hide jealousy and envy under many layers.

They maybe feel guilty in the beginning, but as the feeling evolves they do not care for the signals of the conscience anymore. They feel that their feelings are rightly justified, and then they start to act accordingly. They try to undervalue other people's qualities so theirs can remain floating in the fluffy clouds they created for themselves. And since real greatness will never go around boasting while standing on other people's shoulders and will not fight back unfairly, usually the envious ones get their way. But it still does not satisfy them. Whatever path we choose, we always thrive for more. Evil wants more, and good wants to grow also. Simply by choosing good, there is a benefit of growing and developing more for a high resistance is required. Stagnation is not a law of our mechanism. By choosing inactivity, we are already falling down. Gravity is universal.

Sadly, these people can start to criticize behind people's back, trying to elevate themselves above the person who is a potential harm to their throne of worship. They want the final product, but they did not work hard with honesty and humility to get there. If we look back, great minds and souls were always being attacked by those who were, let's say, not so great.

They do not care to ask questions in sincerity or directly, but they love to sprinkle their own handmade hypotheses about others all around them. My father always said that people are like sheep. One says *beeee*, and all just repeat it. In this case, it happens for the homemade hypothesis with the added rising agent just swelling.

They never thought about the possibility that other folks are not interested in their throne or their cathedra. They are just living their lives.

We do live in a society with a predominant lack of real knowledge, where individual thinking and common sense are developed. And since we cannot claim the medieval ways of keeping people in ignorance, we design hundreds and hundreds of conferences about everything possible and with extrachallenging names and words. That makes them superinviting for the people who did not have a good simple, basic, and profound education to lay their foundation. So instead of really knowing some subject, we became all-knowing sophisticated minds. We repeat the words we heard on that vital or essential life information. We become the kings and queens. We don't want anyone to interfere with our superficial parroted information projected in high-definition on a big screen—so better to eliminate any potential interference.

We could become a highly respected shoe designer, who, if provided the raw material and the tools for making one pair, would not know where to start. Yet because of all the conferences attended and superficial theory, we imagine we could and should be the only shoemaking expert around. Those who perhaps know how to make the shoes but do not have all the pedigrees attached to their names should follow the rules of the experts.

It is my opinion, which does not have to be shared, that none of us knows everything perfectly. We do not have to be envious of anybody. Why aren't the so-called experts with some vision that may be good but isn't based on reality willing to sit and learn hands-on from the old shoemaker? Why not share their thoughts and insights and just develop a nice human-to-human, fellow-to-fellow, mortal-to-mortal conversation and relationship with the old shoemaker opening his views at the same time? We could have older wisdom and experience mixed with new enthusiasm and vision and a much better place to be, without envy and strife. Do you know how the Wars of Roses ended? Henry adopted the Tudor rose as the emblem of England, combining the white rose of York with the red rose of Lancaster to symbolize an end of the wars. Shouldn't we do the same?

All of us have felt the sting of someone's envy or jealousy sometimes in life. It could have been the very refined, stylish, and sophisticated variety or, perhaps, the crude, primitive, and unrefined version. But the sting is painful either way. Maybe we're the ones who caused the wound to others with our own envy. In both cases, we should realize the ugliness of it all just try to stay as far away as possible from those who cannot stand to have someone with ample views and higher aims. And when the feeling of jealousy and envy awakens in our own heart, we should simply destroy it—the very same moment we become aware of it.

Like the Beautiful Castle

Like the castle, time has passed over us, abandoned us, robbed us of the promising dreams we had in our youth. The years have taxed us, and the circumstances haven't always helped. We can still stand. We can stand tall and upright, like the survivors of the bitter and harsh cold winter winds, storms, and ice. There is a beauty in an old castle that did not look like this in the beginning but had some parts added with each new owner. Every phase made it look more like a grand monument of the times passed by. None of us should remain the same. We should add changes to our building constantly—changes toward good and positive. Never is it too late to add some renovation to our old habits. We have to strive toward the best. Mistakes we made can pull us down. But whether we want to remain there or to use the rest of our days doing good is our decision.

The castle has a motto that was not put there from its beginnings. We do not have all the wisdom at the beginning of our journey, but we should strive for it and then add it to the castles of our lives and characters. The motto says *dum spiro, spero* (Latin for "while I breathe, I hope"). For the Spanish-speaking people, it is much easier to understand the relation between the two words *esperar* and *tener esperanza* ("to wait" and "to have hope")—*mientras respiro, espero*. In the Spanish language, there is a saying: "Hay tres cosas que el ser humano necesita en su vida—alguien a quien amar, algo que hacer, y una esperanza para el futuro" (There are three things needed in life—someone to love, something to do, and hope for the future).

While we hope, we are waiting, expecting something better. We can always love others. There are so many broken hearts and lives around us— people who need a real helping hand, a smile that comes from the heart, and kindness that is not faked. While we give to others we are adding a new wing, a new window, a new door, a new tower to our castles. We can always decide to do just the edifying and not the destroying acts. Maybe injustice is too big to bear. Everything in us is screaming for revenge. Should we seek revenge or leave it and focus on doing good? The time is passing. It will keep passing whether we're doing good or bad.

Would it not be better to stand up and start right now to restore our castles? To repair the damage from our own mistakes and our downfall decisions? To do nothing else that will pull us down but, instead, do that which will make us a beacon of hope for others? There is a restoring power in doing good and rising up above our sad circumstances. Some can just leap for it. Some have to start with small baby steps. It is free for all, and we can start right now. There is a beauty to be discovered in that old castle. Let's start now—this very moment.

Conclusion

The first Einstein's wife was born just seventy kilometers from my birthplace. She studied in Switzerland, together with her future husband, and many sources prove that she was his helper and much smarter than him, especially in the field of physics. It did not help in her private life.

The *Titanic* was a floating palace. It was the best and most luxurious ship when it was built and the largest moving human-made object in the world. It didn't not last for long. Its luxury and rich design could not save the human lives onboard after the collision with the iceberg.

I remember watching old movies while growing up and admiring, better said wanting to be like, the beautiful actresses on the big screen. They had such beauty that surely must be the requirement for ultimate happiness in life. Isn't that what movies communicate to us? Just out of curiosity, I wanted to see what happened to all of those shining "stars" years later. How long and sad is the list of broken homes, lives, insecurities and unhappiness. Beauty and fame did not help.

We've heard story after story about Napoleon and Alexander the Great, Attila and Genghis Khan, Julius Cesar and Mark Anthony—the list is centuries long. Power does not extend life.

Knowledge and beauty and power and riches can be very positive if there is something much firmer and truthful behind them—if they will be used for good, if there is a truth we can rely on. There must be a faith and trust that somebody does care for us and that we are not just some free electrons bumping from atom to atom. We need to know that there is purpose, a giver of that purpose, and a reward as well.

We all have to sail in this sea of life. All of us need a chart and knowledge about where we're heading. When sailing under dark and cold night skies, we better know where to look for the lighthouse and not confuse its light with other sources of flashy beams

There are many songs around us. Some have beat that rush the adrenaline levels high, and that is chiefly all we get from them. Many just speak to us in a moment of needing encouragement and to point to something bigger than ourselves. One of the songs from that category that I really appreciate is Ryan Stevenson's "The Eye of the Storm." Many of us know it to be very truthful and real.

Our lives are fragile, our beauty fleeting, our knowledge superficial, and our advances silent in giving genuine happiness. We are created for something more than just to be tossed by the waves here and there. We need not paint on the wall but a real relationship from the heart. We need our own experience. We cannot trade it. It has to be our own testimony. Then we won't need to copy anyone or be insecure. We won't run behind every new theory that is there outside, for we will know for sure what is the truth. We will stand firm, and our compass will always lead us toward the right path.

I was tossed by storms of life—some because of drifting away on my own, some because the tempest came unexpectedly. Some were a waterspout. And there was nice smooth sailing too. So I can say together with Job:

> But as for me, I would seek God,
> And to God I would commit my cause—
> Who does great things, and unsearchable,
> Marvelous things without number.
> He gives rain on the earth,
> And sends waters on the fields.
> He sets on high those who are lowly,
> And those who mourn are lifted to safety.
> He frustrates the devices of the crafty,
> So that their hands cannot carry out their plans.
> He catches the wise in their own craftiness,
> And the counsel of the cunning comes quickly upon them.
> They meet with darkness in the daytime,
> And grope at noontime as in the night.
> But He saves the needy from the sword,
> From the mouth of the mighty,

And from their hand.
So the poor have hope,
And injustice shuts her mouth.
"Behold, happy *is* the man whom God corrects;
Therefore do not despise the chastening of the Almighty.
For He bruises, but He binds up;
He wounds, but His hands make whole.
He shall deliver you in six troubles,
Yes, in seven no evil shall touch you" (Job 5:8–19)

I was again in a new country. I didn't know anyone, and that very first day while sitting and listening to the speaker, I felt that somebody touched my hair. I had long hair back then. The only thing I saw when I turned back was the most beautiful smile of an older lady. At that time, I thought that 60 was old (now I am moving the bar to a 107). That smile was unique, warm, and genuinely kind and welcoming. She became my dear friend and my shoulder for crying. We laughed together, and she and her husband were like my family.

Her husband, who held one of the administrative positions at the university where I had come to study, was the most humble person ever. They were just such a treasure. I don't think that there was anyone who didn't like them, and their big house was always filled with visitors.

After some years, she was terminally ill and, in spite of all the pain and suffering, faith and kindness were still her hallmark. I had my own family, and I would sometimes call her but did not know what to say in those moments of such cruel reality. It was happening so fast.

One day, I came home, and the phone was blinking indicating that there were messages. One message was very difficult to understand the voice was so weak. It was a message from my dear friend encouraging me and sharing her love. She was a firm believer, and she knew that her life had not been spent in vain. Her last words to all her long list of friends and family members were words of encouragement, hope, and love.

My other friend told me that our dear friend had called her too, and many other people reported the same. That was her last day. She spent her last moments doing exactly the same as she had done when she was well—encouraging people, sharing a genuine smile and kindness. She and her husband helped many people, never judging and never gossiping, though she held herself to her own high principles. Her religion was not about holding her principles and beliefs up in to other people's faces but, rather, she lived it.

Bach's life was not a trouble-free life. He became an orphan when he was ten years old. Did you know that the same stone-throwing people we have today were targeting him too? They criticized his music. He had to move a lot. He was not even recognized as a great composer but as an organist. Decades after his life had ended, Felix Mendelssohn rediscovered the copy of the great *St. Matthew Passion*. After that, Bach has become more famous than ever. But he never longed for human greatness. At the bottom of his compositions, we can see a three-letter abbreviation—SDG. He wanted to give glory to God in everything he composed.

There is nothing in us to be much glorified. But if we turn toward the source of all wisdom, our lives can be filled and overflow with a purpose and hope, with love and compassion, with kindness and joy—with peace in the midst of a dark and raging sea—for we know that our lives are in God's hands.

I am still standing in spite of all—because of faith in Him. *Soli Deo gloria* (To the glory of God alone).

Printed in the United States
By Bookmasters